ALLIED
DUNBAR
LIBRARY
MONEY GUIDES

BUYING AND SELLING
YOUR HOME
IN FRANCE

BUYING AND SELLING YOUR HOME IN FRANCE

HENRY DYSON

© Allied Dunbar Financial Services Limited 1991

ISBN 0-85121-732-X

First published 1989
Reprinted 1990

Published by

Longman Law, Tax and Finance
Longman Group UK Limited
21-27 Lamb's Conduit Street, London WC1N 3NJ

Associated Offices

Australia, Hong Kong, Malaysia, Singapore, USA

No responsibility for loss occasioned to any person acting or refraining from action as a result of the material in this publication can be accepted by the author or publishers.

The views and opinions of Allied Dunbar may not necessarily coincide with some of the views and opinions expressed in this book which are solely those of the author and no endorsement of them by Allied Dunbar should be inferred.

A CIP catalogue record for this book is available from the British Library.

Printed and bound in Great Britain by
Biddles Ltd, Guildford and King's Lynn

Foreword

I am delighted to have been given the opportunity by Allied Dunbar and Longman publishers through the medium of the second edition of this book to do my best to help its readers avoid the major pitfalls of buying and building property in France so that they may become happy, trouble-free owners. However, there is much more to reaping the full benefit of home ownership in France, whether it is of a holiday home or of a home in which you live permanently, than avoiding legal pitfalls. You must get to know the French. It is a waste of time and money to buy property in another country and not make some effort to learn its language and understand its people. You must learn how to enjoy all that is best in France of which there is much and how to deal with its less attractive aspects, since France, like every other country, is not exempt from certain character defects.

Living in France by Philip Holland which is published by Robert Hale will in this respect provide an admirable companion to this book. Not only does it cover subjects of which you will need to know more if you decide to buy in France and which are outside the scope of this book but it attempts also to give an insight into why the French behave in the way in which they do. It should therefore help you to extract the maximum pleasure from your home in France.

Contents

1 Introduction   1
What this book is all about   2
Be prepared to seek advice   3
A word of warning   3

2 Where to buy   5
The climate   5
What to buy   6
Where to buy   9
     Côte d'Azur   9
     Provence   9
     The Dordogne   10
     Normandy   10
     Brittany   10
When to house-hunt   12
How to get there   12

3 What to do and what not to do   16
Get advice   16
Watch your budget   17
Look before you buy   19
The legal side   20
A word on tax   20

4 The buying process   22
The contract   22
Seller's commission   26
House purchase loans   27
     Signing   28
The conveyance   28

	Completion	29
	Payment	30
5	**Buying on plan**	32
	The purchase contract	32
	Completion clauses	34
	What to do on the completion of building	35
6	**Financing your purchase**	37
	Background	38
	Using your French Property as security	39
	Using your UK property as security	40
	Currency considerations	41
7	**Building new property**	43
	Some general thoughts	43
	Planning	44
	Do-it-yourself planning	45
	Plan d'occupation des sols	45
	Certificate d'urbanisme	46
	Permis de construire	46
	Certificat de conformité	46
	Building	47
	What not to buy	49
	For discussion with your architect	50
8	**You and French banks**	53
	UK branches	53
	Bank accounts	54
	Rules about cheques	55
	Direct debits	56
	Property purchase loans	57
	Protection of the borrower	57
9	**The French tax system**	59
	The taxes	59
	Resident or non-resident?	60
	Domiciled or not domiciled?	61
	French taxes	61
	Enregistrement	61

French VAT (*Taxe sur la valeur ajoutée–TVA*)   62
Annual taxes on property   63
Income tax   64
Capital gains tax   64
Inheritance tax   64
Offshore companies   67

10   Time-sharing   68
Avoiding problems   68
The costs of time-sharing   69
Some general guidelines   70
Old system *v* new system   71

11   Life in a condominium   74
Costs of flat ownership   74
Systems of flat ownership   75
Obligations and liabilities   76
Service charges   77
What you may and what you may not do   78
Management of the block   78
Meetings   79
Members absent from meetings   81

12   Renting property   82
Points to note   83
Repairs   84
Insurance   84
Service charges   85

13   Settling in   87
Applying for permanent residence   87
Visa de longue durée   88
Carte de séjour   88
Your 'papers'   89
Your car   89
Making the move   89
Importing duty-free goods   90
Using a removal firm   91
Insurance   92

14 Factors to bear in mind   93
Utilities   93
    Water   93
    Electricity   94
    Gas   96
    Telephone   96
    Television   99
    Sewage   99
Running costs and maintenance   99
Insurance   100
Making a claim   102

15 Health and health insurance   103
Reciprocal medical care   103
Medical provision for residents   105
    Sécurité Sociale   106
Medical insurance   106
Provision for death   108

16 French succession law   109
Avoiding the rule   110

17 Making a French Will   113
How many Wills?   113
Why 'ideally' two Wills?   114
The *réserve*   114
Types of French Wills   115
Executors   116
Inheritance tax   117
Final words of advice   118

18 Letting your property   119
Holiday lettings   119
Rules of letting property   120
Long-term lettings   122
General guidelines for letting property   122

19 Selling your property   124
Sale price   124
Estate agents   125

The Mandat	126
Selling Commission	126
Preparing the contract	127
The tax position	128
Completion of the sale	130
The proceeds	131
20 The future	132
Glossary	135
Index	143

1 Introduction

The problems which face the British buyer of property in France are quite different from those which confront buyers of property, for example, in the Iberian Peninsula. France is not a country where property development has taken place specifically with a view to attracting the foreigner although his money is as welcome as that of any other buyer. There are no ghettos where each nationality lives in blocks of flats built by a developer of the same nationality, surrounded by shops and restaurants which depend for their custom on the flat-owners who require to eat the type of food they eat at home and drink the drink imported into the UK and then re-exported with a safe English label into the country from which it came.

If there are problems of property frauds, which today can still frighten the English buyer of property abroad, in France these are often problems in which the buyer has himself knowingly participated in an effort to save himself money. These include cash payments to avoid French VAT and the deliberate insertion of false prices in documents to reduce stamp duties and in both cases it takes two to play the game. Almost all problems stem from not taking proper advice about a legal system which is considerably different from the English system. But it must be said that property frauds do exist, principally in connection with sales 'on plan' and most seem to be perpetrated by non-French developers. It is essential to get advice on this type of purchase.

What this book is all about

The intention of this book is to explain how property —
houses, flats or land — is bought in France. No one should
contemplate buying property without knowing exactly why
they want to do this and, therefore, what it is they should
buy. You should remember that the house market is not a
'tourist' market and that estate agents in France tend to be
very localised in the properties they have on their books.
However, buying through agencies or at exhibitions in the
UK is not necessarily the best way. What you must also
remember (but without in the least being discouraged) is that
you are buying a home in a foreign country and so:

1   the contract you will be asked to sign will be not only in
    French but in legal French and it may be one of a
    number of different types of contracts, and all other
    documents involved will be in similar French,
2   the French legal system is wholly different from the
    English legal system,
3   the French tax system is different from the English tax
    system.

There is no reason to expect that you know any of the rules
but there is every reason to hope that you will take expert
advice about these rules for which, of course, you must be
prepared to pay. You would not try to buy a house in
England without the services of a solicitor and to attempt to
do so abroad without similar assistance is not only foolhardy
but, in the case of purchases in France, can, as you will read
later on, be a grave disservice to your family.

Please remember that this book is intended to help the
private individual and not people buying, selling or letting
property in France on a business basis. For them, there are
special rules — mainly fiscal — and it would be extremely
dangerous to assume that French law does not distinguish in
connection with land transactions between the 'professional'

and the 'non-professional'. It does, in some respects, quite severely.

Be prepared to seek advice

You have taken the first step; you have bought this book. The question is where do you go now for the kind of advice you will need to make certain that the pitfalls are avoided? What must you do to make certain that your purchase is not only properly dealt with from a French legal point of view but takes into account, if it is of a holiday home, that you are still living in England or, if it is a retirement home, of your British nationality and background. Ideally, the person to advise you is someone with a considerable knowledge of and practical experience in both English and French law who preferably lives in France. It may be that your own solicitor has such a contact but one of the best alternative sources of information in England is the Solicitors Property Group which has a section dealing with French property purchases or in France, either the local British Consul or the manager of one of the local 'British' banks. Either of these will know the person they recommend and the extent of their experience. This is of considerable importance because in all probability you will be advised to give that person a power of attorney to act for you on completion and generally to look after your interests.

A word of warning

French consumer protection law covers a wide variety of situations and much of it relating to property purchases and building goes back a number of years. The French legal system is incredibly slow: often it will take two years for a case to get to court and about 50% of all cases go to appeal, taking at least another two years. In theory, there is likely to be a rule or regulation available to deal with most of what could go wrong in the majority of cases. The difficulty is that theory is not practice. The moral is, if you cannot avoid every problem, at least avoid as many as you can by taking the right advice from the right person from the very beginning.

This book is intended to help you by taking a look at the matters you should bear in mind when you are about to become involved in property transactions in France. It is written in general terms and so is not meant to take the place of specific advice about a particular situation. Do not treat it as a DIY guide to buying and selling French property. It is hoped that it will be of general interest and help you to avoid the pitfalls and understand the advice which you have wisely sought.

It is very difficult to say what, if any, changes will follow in the wake of the much heralded year 1992. It is certain that in some respects France, like other countries, is adopting rules and regulations common to all EC countries. Equally, where these rules and regulations do not suit the French, they opt out of them as often as do other countries. In general terms, it seems unlikely that for some time to come, the French legal system, insofar as buying and selling property is concerned, will undergo any substantial change. However, the next few years are obviously years of change generally and the need to check the written word cannot be too strongly emphasised in order to make sure that no change has taken place since publication.

2 Where to buy

From holidays taken in France over many years or from business trips, you may have a very good idea where in France you wish to buy your property. Nevertheless, it is just as well to calmly think through the factors which ought to be taken into account at the start of your property search.

The climate

Paris is taken to be the norm when discussing the climate in France and this is about the same as the climate in London. You have to go at least as far south as the Loire to find a gentler climate, which tends to be wetter in the west and drier in the east. An exception to this is a small part of Normandy around Dieppe and Brittany which enjoys a climate very similar to parts of southern Cornwall or the west of Ireland, ie it is mild but extremely rainy.

The area to the east of Bordeaux — Bergerac and the Dordogne which are very popular with the British — has long warm summers but is rainy and foggy in winter. Further south along the Atlantic coast, in the south-west corner of France, the weather is warmer in summer but just as wet in winter, with a cold Atlantic Ocean to bathe in.

The Massif Central acts as a barrier between north and south so that, south of this mountainous range, there are long hot summers and short wet winters. The mistral, a cold gap wind, blows down the Rhone valley affecting the whole of southern and western Provence and the Tramontane blows in the Rousillon-Longuedoc region. Except for the area between Narbonne and Montpellier, where they can be very fierce, these winds are a minor irritant but should be taken into account. Finally, there is the area known as the Midi, stretching from the Pyrenees to the Alps (which includes the Rousillon-Longuedoc, a part of Provence and all the Côte d'Azur) which is hot and dry except for a couple of months in early spring when the annual rains fall, sometimes heavily.

What to buy

There is a wide range of properties available, whose prices vary enormously depending not only on the kind of property involved but the area in which it is situated. There is land available for building whatever house the planners will allow you to build and there are building estates run as condominiums where either you buy a plot of land and build or have built for you a house in accordance with whatever overall planning consent has been obtained for the estate. There are new houses and old houses, town houses and village houses. There are new flats and old flats. There are *mas* and there are *châteaux* — dilapidated and ripe for renovation or already restored. There is no limit to what is available but each kind of property has its own special attractions and problems. Building land is dealt with in Chapter 7.

When it comes to existing houses and flats, you must be careful with the meaning of the word 'new'. New tends to mean either that a property is brand new and you will be the first owner or that it has been completed within the last five years and the sale to you would qualify for a reduced rate of stamp duty (see Chapter 9). It is customary for estate agents to refer to a sale of property to a buyer who is not the first owner as a *revente* but this does not mean that you will not benefit from low stamp duty.

Flats have a vocabulary of their own. *Grand luxe* and *'grand standing'* are similar to 'luxury' or 'high class' in England. *Vue imprenable* is intended to suggest a view (of the sea, mountains etc) which will endure for ever. In fact, it means that the existing view is clear of obstruction but promises nothing as to the future. Flats built some years ago in the turn-of-the-century style with high ceilings, large rooms and vast windows are known as *bourgeois* or 'monied class'. Unless they have been modernised, they will have fairly undesirable bathrooms and kitchens and probably any room which is not a 'public' room will be dowdy. This is because the French — and particularly the French bourgeoisie — are very anxious to make a good impression on visitors at the expense of what the visitors do not see. These flats have a certain charm but will be expensive to decorate, furnish and upkeep.

More modern flats have smaller rooms but the standard of building will certainly be less high than with older flats. The most modern will have individual heating and hot water. Avoid those that do not since you will find that your service charges will include the cost of heating other people's flats and providing other people with hot water. Do not worry too much about stamp duty being low on very new flats and high on older flats. On the whole, the fact that stamp duty is low on new flats tempts developers to charge buyers that bit more than they otherwise could. Modern flats are available from a studio design to those with five rooms. Remember that the French describe flats by the number of rooms and not by the number of bedrooms and that prices increase the higher it is situated in a block.

Remember also that it is axiomatic that all new blocks of flats will suffer from problems. Not just faulty workmanship which ultimately can be put right at the cost of the developer or some insurance company but, for example, a lack of suitable security arrangements. This may not have been apparent when you (and many other buyers) decided to buy a flat in that block. When it is finally decided to instal what the developer did not instal, the capital cost will be reflected in your service charge.

The *mas* is a farmhouse in the south and south-west of France. There is a certain chic about owning one. Indeed, they are sought-after and relatively expensive. It is not easy to find one for restoration but they do exist. Not only will you need expert architectural help but also builders and other tradesmen whom you can trust to begin, carry on and finish the work. The average *mas* is exactly where you would expect a farm to be and hence can be very unpleasant in winter if there are holes in the walls, no central heating and ill-fitting windows because your builders have failed to keep to their completion date.

A *château* can be anything from a real Loire castle to a large country house in good, poor or dilapidated condition. They are to be found all over France and the genuine ones are those which are in the right style for the place where they are built. Among the most attractive but, alas, rare are the *gentilhommières* to be found throughout the country other than Provence and principally in Languedoc and the Ile de France. These are small 18th-century houses built for the gentry and usually have some six to eight bedrooms and numerous rooms on the ground floor.

Prices vary according to the part of the country where the property is and the condition in which it is in. As with the English manor or court house, anything fashionable or sought-after is expensive. Beware the tumbledown farmhouse and the property 'suitable for restoration'; it is likely to be offered at a price which is unreasonable in France even if it seems cheap by current English standards. Anything really of interest will, apart from being expensive, possibly carry with it the problem of being a listed building since the French control these both indoors as well as outdoors.

Where to buy

Côte d'Azur

For well over 100 years the Côte d'Azur has been the happy hunting ground for the British buyer. It stretches from Menton to La Napoule but the area has been extended westward to include St Tropez as more and more villages on the coast have been developed. Along the coast as far as Marseilles is a series of resorts and villages, many with marinas, which are particularly attractive to yachtsmen. They vary considerably in price and quality: of those to the east of Nice, Cap Ferrat, Beaulieu and Villefranche are probably the most attractive and expensive. Nice and Cannes are certainly not cheap either, but Cannes is the more expensive.

Provence

Parallel to the South coast but some miles inland is a string of Provençal villages, some of which are particularly attractive and some of which have suffered from the tourist trade. In this area are also 'two season' villages and small towns, equally attractive in summer and available for skiing in winter. The motorway from Aix en Provence to the frontier at Menton runs parallel to the coast on average 10 to 15 miles away until, close to Cannes, it comes almost down to the sea. The Var, which is the *département* through which it passes before reaching Cannes, is a delightful area and it is well worth while thinking of land for building between the motorway and the coast as well as north of the motorway into deep country.

The area between Toulouse and the Gulf of Lion contains the wine lake of France. Hot and dry in summer, the coastal area in the Roussillon-Longuedoc has special charm. Property prices here are much lower than on the Côte d'Azur and they tend to drop the further north you go. This is becoming an increasingly popular area, depending on the airports at

Toulouse and Montpellier and the départements of Ardèche, Aveyron, Gard, Herault and Lozère are seeing an influx of British, German and Dutch buyers. There can be some climatic difficulties which can be measured; the more important difficulty for the non-French buyer in country districts is that there is available virtually no legal knowledge of a standard sufficient to deal with the needs of the non-French buying French property.

The Dordogne

Further north along the Atlantic coast is Bordeaux which is considerably less hot than the south of France and is where the airport for the Dordogne is situated. It has a charm of its own, delicious food and quite interesting wines but a less interesting climate.

Normandy

Currently, interest seems centred on the more northern parts of France which are said to be within easy reach of the mouth of the Channel Tunnel. Property prices in these areas are for the moment lower than those in some other parts of the country.

Sufficient time has now passed since the decision to build the Tunnel coupled with the realisation by the French that property in the north could be sold to the English at inflated prices to permit second thoughts. It is perhaps still too early to know whether the author's view that this is not the part of France in which to buy, is justified or not; suffice it to say that this area has not proved an attraction in the past to those who have no need for a tunnel to reach it.

Brittany

This area is very attractive to the British and indeed the countryside and half-timbered houses recall the south and west parts of England. Alas, the climate is also very similar and this part of France has a very high rainfall. The local language is incomprehensible to anyone but the Breton who spends a lot of time attempting to secede from France. The local cuisine is excellent and, exceptionally, the standard butter is salted. Motorways and fast trains are a useful new addition to the scene.

Figure 1: The regions and départements of France

Source: French Government Tourist Office

When to house-hunt

Two weeks' holiday is not enough to judge whether you will like a particular area or property. It is vital to see your chosen area of purchase at all times of the year but especially in high summer and mid-winter. A great number of northern Europeans find they cannot take the full brunt of a Mediterranean summer and cannot cope with shopping and household chores in the heat. For these people the more central or westerly parts of France would be the answer. Spring and autumn are delightful seasons throughout France but, at higher altitudes, spring can arrive relatively late and autumn can start surprisingly early, often in the second week of September.

Those purchasing flats where the block has a pool would do well to estimate in advance how many people could be using the pool in high summer. What looks charming and large in April can turn out to be pathetically inadequate in August. You will, of course, want your house guests to be able to use the pool, as will all the other *co-propriétaires* and it needs little imagination to realise how very crowded the pool area can become.

How to get there

France has many airports into which fly both international and national airlines. There are direct flights from various airports in the UK to destinations all over France and there is a continuous shuttle service from Heathrow to Paris. Charter flights to certain airports abound during the tourist season but fares from the UK may seem unreasonably high. The airport at Marseilles is not often offered as a suitable place to use but it is far more convenient than Nice Airport for the western end of the south coast. The airports at Montpellier, Toulouse, and Lyons may not regularly be served direct from the UK and may not benefit from charter flights but by using them you may save yourself time, since they can easily be reached via Paris.

Road travel in France presents very few problems. There is a vast network of motorways and a well-maintained system of main and secondary roads. More and more motorways are being built and much of France is now, in normal conditions, within an easy day's drive from Paris. Remember, however, that all traffic from the north of Europe to Spain and Portugal passes through France, as does traffic on its way to parts of Italy. Therefore, at the height of the season, both in summer and in winter, traffic conditions can be very difficult on some of the motorways.

France also boasts an excellent railway system which enables you to put a car on a train and sleep through the night instead of driving from the Channel coast to the south and west. There are also a number of high-speed trains which cross the country remarkably quickly. On the whole, rail travel is not expensive and many special reductions are available.

There are, nevertheless, certain things worth remembering when travelling in France. As you would expect, all estate agents underestimate the time it takes to get from any point of arrival to the house they want to sell. You can discover the truth only by completing the journey yourself. There are also certain places which although they are quite close to airports or motorways can be, at the height of the tourist season, extremely tedious to reach because of the large number of people travelling in these areas. Getting to and from a holiday home is an important point, particularly if you have children, and, if you are setting up permanently in France, local communications are as important as they are in the UK.

No mention has been made of Monaco because it is not part of France. Becoming a resident in Monaco can have certain advantages but, except in rather special cases, if you plan to live there because of the tax savings, you are liable to find that the cost of living is such that what you hope to save on tax you will spend on cups of coffee. Monaco has its own rules and regulations with regard to property and virtually nothing of what you read in this book applies to that principality.

Figure 2: Code Numbers of French *Départements* (Counties)

01 — Ain
02 — Aisne
03 — Allier
04 — Alpes de Haute Provence
05 — Hautes-Alpes
06 — Alpes-Maritimes
07 — Ardèche
08 — Ardennes
09 — Ariège
10 — Aube
11 — Aude
12 — Aveyron
13 — Bouches-du-Rhône
14 — Calvados
15 — Cantal
16 — Charente
17 — Charente-Maritime
18 — Cher
19 — Corrèze
20 — Corse
21 — Côte-d'Or
22 — Côtes-du-Nord
23 — Creuse
24 — Dordogne
25 — Doubs
26 — Drôme
27 — Eure
28 — Eure-et-Loir
29 — Finistère
30 — Gard
31 — Haute-Garonne
32 — Gers

33 — Gironde
34 — Hérault
35 — Ille-et-Vilaine
36 — Indre
37 — Indre-et-Loire
38 — Isère
39 — Jura
40 — Landes
41 — Loir et Cher
42 — Loire
43 — Haute-Loire
44 — Loire-Atlantique
45 — Loiret
46 — Lot
47 — Lot-et-Garonne
48 — Lozère
49 — Maine-et-Loire
50 — Manche
51 — Marne
52 — Haute-Marne
53 — Mayenne
54 — Meurthe-et-Moselle
55 — Meuse
56 — Morbinhan
57 — Moselle
58 — Nièvre
59 — Nord
60 — Oise
61 — Orne
62 — Pas-de-Calais
63 — Puy-de-Dôme
64 — Pyrénées-Atlantiques

65 — Hautes-Pyrénées
66 — Pyrénées-Orientales
67 — Bas-Rhin
68 — Haut-Rhin
69 — Rhône
70 — Haut-Saône
71 — Saône-et-Loire
72 — Sarthe
73 — Savoie
74 — Haute-Savoie
75 — Paris
76 — Seine-Maritime
77 — Seine-et-Marne
78 — Yvelines
79 — Deux-Sèvres
80 — Somme
81 — Tarn
82 — Tarn-et-Garonne
83 — Var
84 — Vaucluse
85 — Vendée
86 — Vienna
87 — Haute-Vienne
88 — Vosges
89 — Yonne
90 — Territoire-de-Belfort
91 — Essonne
92 — Hauts-de-Seine
93 — Seine-Saint-Denis
94 — Val-de-Marne
95 — Val-d'Oise

3 What to do and what not to do

In this chapter you will find some important points which you should bear in mind when you are buying property in France. The basic problem is that most English buyers of property in France are used to the English system where they have been guided through the trauma of house purchase by their solicitors. There is no equivalent to this service in France. The system expects you, in the majority of cases, to sign a contract prepared by an estate agent virtually without any previous enquiries and without the services of a surveyor. You are expected to make your own mortgage arrangements and also to sign a complicated purchase document in front of a notary who (quite properly) is often also acting for the seller. Finally, you will normally have to deal with the insurance of the property when you have bought it, when you are used to your solicitor doing this automatically for you.

Get advice

Do not be put off in any way by all this. The solution is to entrust your purchase to a suitable adviser (preferably in France) who will look after your interests as far as possible as though you were buying in England.

Think of what you would do if you were buying property in the UK. You would:

1   not necessarily buy the first house or flat you saw,

2 not sign a contract presented to you by the seller's agent but arrange for it to be sent to your solicitor,
3 work out carefully your financial situation and consult your bank manager or accountant or solicitor, to see if you could afford the price asked and how you could best raise it,
4 if you were buying with a mortgage loan, get the offer of that loan before exchanging contracts or make the contract conditional on that offer,
5 if what you were buying was a 'second home', get your tax position clarified.

When you had decided that the house was what you were looking for and that you could afford it, you would go ahead in the knowledge that your solicitor would protect you from all legal problems.

Similar rules apply to buying property in France. However, the French cannot normally get all this advice from one person and have to do some of the work themselves. The solution is to treat yourself to the same sort of protection as you would in England. Added to this, there is the obvious problem that even if you speak French reasonably well, you probably do not speak legal and technical French. Therefore, you may find it difficult to negotiate and to get the kind of information you need to help you make decisions.

Remember that although fraudulent builders are rare, bankrupt builders are quite common. Do not sign building contracts given to you by builders without advice (would you do so in England?) and do not use architects recommended to you by builders. Let your chosen expert in France check out both architect and builder.

Watch your budget

You must bear in mind that buying (and selling) property in France can in many circumstances be more expensive than in the UK. Selling agents tend to charge approximately 5% commission. Although this is in most parts of France payable by the seller, it is sometimes added on to the asking price so that it is the buyer who pays commission. On the other hand, whilst in limited circumstances new property carries a very reduced rate of stamp duty, a purchase outside this range will involve fees and disbursements of approximately 10%, of which stamp duty is a large proportion. Non-residents may also have to pay capital gains tax, currently at the rate of 33.3%. Hence, changing houses can be expensive and it is worth while making the right choice first time round depending on your probable future plans: a holiday home that will always remain a holiday home, or something which can become a retirement home, or perhaps just a plot of land which can be built on in the future.

Never over-commit yourself. Wild fluctuations in the sterling/franc rate are rare but, as the minimum time between finding your property and completing will probably not be less than two months changes in the exchange rate are likely. If you are buying on 'plan' a flat or house which has not yet been completed, you will probably have to spread stage payments over at least a year. A turn against the franc could cause problems and you should get advice from your bank manager on how best to guard against this risk.

Remember that basically French legal costs and disbursements must be assumed to be about 10% of the purchase price. In certain cases, they can be much less but they could be higher and they *have* to be produced on or before completion. Do not rely on friends' estimations of costs: there are so many factors to take into account that there can be wide variations from purchase to purchase.

Remember also that if you have a French mortgage and your income to service it comes from the UK, you may have a long-term, two-country inflation problem to cope with as well as an exchange rate problem. The same applies for ordinary outgoings and, if you have bought a flat, for your service charges.

Look before you buy

It is a safe rule to rely upon that in any country the second house you see is more suitable than the first. Do not be 'pushed' by selling agents; it is highly unlikely that you will lose your 'dream' flat if you do not sign immediately. In any case, no contract should be signed before you have taken proper independent advice.

Although there appear to be few if any inspection flights to France, it is often worth paying a second visit to the property you think you will buy before making a final decision. If at this stage you contact the right person in France for advice, they will be able to 'keep warm' the property for you for a reasonable period. If, after careful thought, you make your decision to buy while you are in England, contracts can be signed on your behalf without your returning to France.

Ideally, you should see the property that you are going to buy in the worst possible conditions. It does rain even in the south of France and during at least three months of the year it can be chilly as well. If you are thinking of buying in the north, make certain that the fact that the climate can be every bit as unpleasant as in the UK has weighed sufficiently with you. At least for the next few years, treat with reserve the time schedules for Channel Tunnel travel. In the south of France, every piece of property is said to be within a maximum of 40 minutes of Nice Airport! It is probable that the same convenient underestimate will be used by sellers and their agents in the north. Best of all, if you are buying a permanent home, it pays to spend a few months in France just looking around. Why not rent a flat for a short while and do this at your leisure?

The legal side

It is important to engage the services of the right kind of
adviser in France. You will probably get the best advice from
a suitably qualified English person living in France and with
a knowledge of French law and who has also practised in
England.

Do not sign anything without consulting the adviser you have
chosen to look after your interests and never pay over money
without his advice. If you feel that you must make some
payment without being covered in this way, only make
payments in favour of a notary.

If you are offered documents which have been translated into
English to consider at your leisure, be extremely wary of
what they say. Some will be in bad English but the most
dangerous are those which are in reasonably good English but
put French legal terms into what the translator thought were
the equivalent English legal terms. Some results are amusing
but others are terribly misleading.

A word on tax

You need not worry that all taxes due on the completion of a
purchase in France will not be paid. It is the duty of the
notary to see that this is done and he incurs jointly with you
a personal liability to see that this happens. That is why he
will never complete until he has in hand all the cash
necessary to enable him to make these payments. Annual
taxes in respect of French property are normally payable in
arrears at the end of the year. You usually have about two
months in which to pay, after which time 10% is added to the
bill.

France is not a tax haven for people who cheat. Putting false values in documents for property will land you in trouble. Do not accept that it is safe or easy to do this; it is not true and the person who is trying to persuade you otherwise will almost certainly be the one who stands to benefit and you will be the one who stands to suffer.

4 The buying process

In France, as in England, buying property falls into two parts: the contract and the conveyance. Essentially, in both countries the object is to see that you get what you have agreed to buy, that it brings with it no surprises, that it serves the purpose for which it was sold to you and that you get a good title to it. The way in which the French system sets about this is rather different from how it is done in England.

The contract

In England, when you have found the house you like, you tell the estate agent to send details to your solicitor and you pay him a visit. He gets in touch with the seller's solicitor who sends him a draft of the contract. He then asks certain questions and, when he is satisfied with all the answers and with what the contract says, he explains it all to you and asks you to sign it. The seller then signs his part of the contract and the deal is done.

Not so in France. The normal procedure is for the seller's estate agent to prepare the contract, which is often in standard form, and to hand it to the buyer for his signature. The buyer usually signs without question if the price is right and the date for completion is satisfactory. In many cases, no great harm is done by following this procedure if you are buying a flat in one of the large cities, but if you are buying land or any kind of property elsewhere, and *in particular in the country*, you should always get advice before signing anything. There are good reasons for this:

1   There are a number of different kinds of document loosely called contracts. The most usual and satisfactory is the *compromis de vente* which, like the English contract, is signed by both parties and binds both parties from the moment of signature. There are also documents which you might reasonably think were binding contracts but which are nothing more than offers to sell or to buy and have no value at all until the offer has been accepted by the buyer or the seller, as the case may be. Even then, many contracts of this kind are void if not lodged for stamping (*enregistré*) within quite a short time. The type of contract used is partly a question of local usage and partly of what the selling agent normally uses or thinks he wants to use. Whilst it is not recommended that you sign even a straightforward *compromis de vente* without advice, you should *never* sign any other type of contract without getting advice.

2   It is not unusual for agents to prepare contracts without having seen the seller's title deeds. This means that the property you are buying may be wrongly described and important details may be missing. This is bad enough with a flat in a block but in the case of country properties and land itself, this is dangerous. A full description should appear and, except in the simplest cases, insist on an up to date cadastral plan.

3   Watch out for deposits. Usually they are of the order of 10% and this is reasonable if completion is not delayed. Always pay deposits to your notary, or the seller's notary, and not to the estate agent. This is not because the seller's estate agent or notary is not to be trusted although obviously no payment should ever be made to an estate agent if he is not the holder of a *carte professionelle* (see Chapter 19). It is because, if things go wrong, and you become or think you have become entitled to the return of your deposit, it is going to be much more difficult to get it back from the seller's agent or notary than from

your own notary. There are three types of deposit and what happens to them if either party defaults depends on which type they are. Usually, the contract will contain a penalty clause so that if the buyer defaults he will lose his deposit or the amount of the penalty if it is higher. If the seller defaults, he will pay the penalty amount. It is important to seek advice about this.

4   Most contracts offered to you to sign give the name of the notary who is to prepare the *acte de vente* and, in most cases, it will be the seller's notary. You must never accept this and insist on inserting the name of your own notary as well. This is your *absolute right*. You can instruct your own notary up to the day of completion, even if the contract contains only the name of the seller's notary. However, if you leave it too long after exchange of contracts, it becomes embarrassing for the notary you finally instruct since the seller's notary will have done most or all of the work and the notary instructed by you will find it difficult to insist on an equal share of the notarial fee. It must be admitted that it is not unknown for seller's notaries not instructed to act for buyers, deliberately to fail to get in touch with the notary instructed to act for the buyer. The practice is not common but it exists, especially in rural areas and must be stamped out. It is you who pays the notarial fee in any event and, if there are two notaries involved, they share a single fee.

5   Watch out for the clause about commission, which is dealt with separately below.

6   Some contracts provide for both parties to be liable for commission if the sale goes off by mutual agreement. This may seem surprising but so many French sellers try to avoid paying their agents' commission by conniving with the buyer to cancel the contract and then going quietly to the notary to complete the deal that it is hard not to advise the honest buyer to agree to this.

7   It is rare for completion dates to be fixed but they are usually on an 'on or before' basis to allow time for searches and enquiries to be completed. This means that a deposit may be lying around for a long time when it could

be retained by the buyer and earning interest. It is worth
asking your bank to block the amount in a deposit
account and to give a letter to the seller saying that it will
irrevocably hand over the cash when it becomes due.
Some banks will do this and some sellers will agree to it.

8 Most searches are made after contracts have been signed
so that contracts tend to be subject to rather general
conditions that nothing untoward will turn up. Generally,
property is sold subject to the condition that it is taken in
the state it is on completion. Therefore, take note of
anything that happens between contracts and completion.

9 Every contract other than a contract for the purchase of
property 'on plan' *must* contain a statement by the buyer
to say whether he is buying with the aid of a loan or not
(see below).

10 If you are buying a flat in a condominium or a property
on a *lotissement*, a copy of the *règlement de copropriété*
should be made available with the contract *before*
completion. It is also useful to have a copy of the last
service charge account.

It is important to know that unlike English law, French law
allows a valid contract for the sale of land to be verbal only.
From a practical point of view, few sellers would be content
to rely on such an arrangement because of the obvious
difficulties of proving such a contract. However, a contract
for the sale of any object, be it land or a pin cushion, is a
binding contract provided the subject matter has been clearly
identified and the price agreed. Moreover, as between the
parties to that agreement, the sale is concluded at that
moment, and the property in the goods or land passes to the
buyer. In the case of land, this is of little significance, since
until the transaction is registered at the Land Registry, it has
no effect on third parties.

Many notaries offer *Assurance Automatique Acquéreur* free of
cost to purchasers. This covers the contracting purchaser for
up to one million francs should he die or suffer total
disability from an accident before completion. This insurance

is automatic, costs nothing and needs no medical examination provided that:

1   the contract was signed before a notary (thus the standard estate agents' contracts do not attract this benefit),
2   the contract must be registered or must be accompanied by the payment to a notary of a deposit of at least 5% of the purchase price, and,
3   the purchaser must not be aged more than 65.

The beneficiary of the policy moneys may be the purchaser or his successors in title or any other person named in the contract.

Seller's commission

The general rule in France is that the seller pays his selling agent's commission. This rule can, of course be varied by agreement between the parties. In certain parts of France, by tradition, either the commission is split between seller and buyer or it is paid by the buyer alone.

Unfortunately, it is not possible to say which these areas are since neither the estate agents nor the notaries outside these areas have any list of the places where these exceptions apply. On the whole, they are country areas in the south-west and west of the country, certain areas in the north and the whole of Alsace but this is not an exclusive list. The general rule applies throughout the south.

An additional difficulty is that in many places, it is the notaire and not an estate agent who negotiates the sale and in addition makes every effort to act also for the buyer ie prepares a contract which shows himself as the sole notary involved without advising the buyer of his right in this respect. In cases where the seller's notary acts also as selling agent, the commission is treated as part of the *frais d'acte* and as such is payable by the buyer. In such a case, the scale commission is 5% on the first 175,000 francs and 2½% on the balance of the price. It follows that in areas where this practice pertains, the lower the value of the property, the higher the percentage proportion of the total cost of purchase which in some cases can be exorbitant.

A further difficulty is that in a number of cases, the buyer will have instructed an agent in the UK to find him a property so that he may incur a 'finder's fee' and also the seller's commission and find that he has as notary the same person who not only acts for the seller but actually negotiated the sale from the seller to him.

All this is avoidable. There may in principle be no reason not to use the services of English estate agents when buying French property, but in practice this is not a course of action to be adopted without seeking the most careful legal advice from someone conversant with the practice in France. In any event *never sign any contract* in a purchase organised in this way without such advice.

House purchase loans

Every contract other than a purchase of property 'on plan' to buy a property must state whether the buyer is obtaining a loan to help towards the price. If he is, then the contract is automatically subject to the condition that he gets his loan and he is allowed a minimum of one month from the date of the contract to do so, although the period may be longer if the seller agrees. If he genuinely fails to obtain a loan, he may cancel the contract and will be reimbursed any money he has paid under it. It is obvious that no seller will agree to sell to a buyer who needs to get a loan which is unreasonably large or which the seller suspects that the buyer cannot obtain for one reason or another. It is no use for a buyer who wants to find an excuse to 'cry off' failing to look for a loan.

Provided that it is on normal terms, the seller can find a loan for him and this will fulfil the condition. If a buyer states in the contract that he is not seeking a loan, he cannot at a later stage rely on this statutory condition. See Chapter 8 on mortgages.

Signing

Take note of the date of your contract: many contracts are signed on different dates by the seller and the buyer, but make certain that the contract is given the date of the last signature.

A *compromise de vente* should be in as many original copies as there are parties if this requirement is not fulfilled, the contract is void. There is no harm in parties adding a *mention* such as *vu et approuvé bon pour* . . . in front of their signatures but it is absolutely unneccessary except in certain circumstances, which the average buyer or seller of land will never encounter.

If you are thinking of buying 'on plan' see Chapter 5.

The conveyance

The transfer of land in France is by an *acte de vente* or conveyance. Strictly speaking, a sale of land is complete between seller and buyer as soon as the contract is signed but it remains ineffective as against everyone else until registered at the *Bureau des Hypothèques*. Since for fiscal reasons only a notarial document can be so registered, the contract is 'repeated' in this form at completion. The *acte de vente* is usually a document many pages long, much of which is photocopied from the previous conveyance to the seller. This is one of the reasons why a buyer ought to use his own and not the seller's notary, for otherwise the same notary simply goes from one sale to another never rechecking the title since he first dealt with it.

It is pointless a buyer trying to go through an *acte de vente* in France. It will be quite beyond him. A buyer has therefore a number of choices: he lets the seller's notary act for him and takes a risk or he chooses his own notary but in either case he will probably not be given much explanation before or at completion and he may have difficulty in understanding much of what he is told. His third choice is to seek advice and appoint an adviser as his attorney, leaving it to him to vet everything and explain the procedure to him in his own language and in terms he can understand.

This last choice is ideal and really only coincides with what a buyer would be doing in England. If you appoint your own notary but do not take further advice, it is not so much that there is a risk of not getting good title to what you are buying; that you will probably get, but think of all the questions you ask your solicitor when you buy a home in England and all the advice you get from him. Would you be happy to do without that? There is no reason why you should deprive yourself of this valuable advice when you buy a home outside of England.

Completion

As a buyer attempting to deal with a purchase on your own, it is highly improbable that you will hear anything until you receive from the notary involved a letter giving you a date for completion. You will not, as in England, be advised from time to time of progress. The notary may assume that you are coming in person to complete or he may assume that you are appointing an attorney. The rule is that all parties to a notarial document must be present in person or represented by an attorney.

If you have asked a local adviser to act for you, he will keep you informed of the progress of purchase and, in due course, will send you a Power of Attorney. If you get a Power of Attorney directly from the notary, you would be wise not to use it. It will almost certainly appoint one of his clerks to be your attorney and this merely ensures that if all your requirements have not been complied with, or if there are any problems, there is no independent person to complain on your behalf. Worse still, it will probably contain a blank for the name of the Attorney and it is certain that you would never agree to sign a blank Power in England. Also, your attorney, who should be acting in your interests alone, is an employee of the notary. Even at this late stage, if you have not sought advice before, seek it now. This does not mean that notaries cannot be trusted but that the French system of one notary for both parties is potentially dangerous, particularly if someone in his office is also acting as an attorney for you.

Payment

Although there are no exchange control rules about foreigners buying French property there it is not advisable to send cash needed for completion direct to the notary. Again, this is not because he cannot be trusted but because the cash will take a long time to arrive and on the the way will spend nights in various French banks earning interest for the French Government. Even when it arrives in the notary's account, it is in a special State bank where all notaries are obliged to have their clients' accounts and, if completion is delayed, it is M. le President de la Republique Française who is that much richer. It is preferable to open your own bank account so that the cash can stay on deposit there earning money for you until your local adviser, who will also be your attorney, is given a draft in favour of the notary on the day of actual completion.

The amount required on or before completion will include notarial fees, stamp duties and other disbursements. There is no 'completion statement' as there is in England. No problems arise on the registration of the conveyance to you as this is undertaken by your notary but usually there is no rush to do this. The registration procedure takes weeks or months depending on which local Land Registry is involved but it is not registration which perfects the transaction between you and the seller. It merely gives notice that you are now the owner of the property you have bought so that the tax authorities can collect *taxe foncière* or land tax from you.

In due course, you will receive the *expédition* or certified copy of your title document from your notary. Original title documents do not exist, that is to say, they are kept in the notary's records. There are no problems in France of properties which do not exist or non-existent title deeds such as have plagued buyers in Spain. There are sometimes problems about who owns a property because, unlike the English Land Registry, registration does not guarantee title. That is why you must have a notary separate from the seller's notary so that, when you buy, a single notary who investigates the title he offers to himself is not the only protection you have.

There are a number of local procedural variations in France. The procedure mentioned above is 'standard' but you must not be surprised if it does not follow exactly what you are asked to do.

5 Buying on plan

Buying 'on plan' or *l'état futur d'achèvement* is a common way of buying new flats or apartments in France. There is no reason why you should not buy a house in this way but since more flats than houses are being built, it is less common.

The advantages of this method of buying are that:

1 you pay for your flat over a period of time rather than by one single payment, which may make things easier for you,
2 to some extent, it gives you the chance to choose interior decoration,
3 so far as the design of the building allows, you may also be able to change around the interior of your flat. Normally alterations of this kind will increase the price.

You will, of course, be told that you are buying tomorrow's flat at today's price but it seems improbable that the developer has not taken account of what tomorrow's price will be. You also suffer from the possible disadvantage that quite a large percentage of buildings are not completed on time.

The purchase contract

There is a very strict Law to protect people who buy in this way. The purchase contract is called, rather misleadingly for the British, a *contract de réservation* or sometimes a *contract préliminare*. This is not a reservation for you with the developer of a flat until you are ready to sign a contract to buy it but is itself a contract which binds you to buy. You will lose your deposit if you fail to complete. The contract must contain:

1 a full description of the property to be sold plus outline specifications of the work which will be done. These should include references to domestic services to be supplied. The specifications are in fairly technical French or at least refer to types of French materials and equipment. Try to have these checked by an English surveyor or someone who can translate and explain,

2 the price together with a statement as to whether it is to be a firm price or subject to revision. Most prices are firm but if they can be varied, this must be in accordance with one of two indices, of which the Cost of Construction index is the more usual,

3 the time at which stage payments are to be made. These will be made on presentation of architect's certificates. The Law sets out what percentage of the price may be asked for at each stage. These are maximum payments and developers may (and often do) ask for more frequent and smaller payments but they must not ask for more than the legal maximum at any given stage,

4 the amount of the deposit (*réservation*). This may not exceed 5% if the sale is to be completed within one year or 2% if the delay is to be two years. Longer than that and no deposit may be taken. Deposits must be paid either to a notary or to a special blocked account with a bank,

5 Under the Law of the 31 December 1989, every non-notarial contract for a purchase *en l'état futur d'achèvement* by a non-professional buyer takes effect only after the expiry of seven days from its receipt by registered AR post by the buyer during which period he may 'cry off'. This right must also be exercised by registered AR post, the date of receipt being the relevant date.

Completion Clauses

Completion of the purchase as opposed to completion of the building works will be provided for in the contract. The Law requires that some of its clauses are repeated in the contract of which the most important are:

1   you may ask for the return of your deposit if the developer does not sign the conveyance to you by the date mentioned in the contract,
2   you may also ask for the return of your deposit if on coming to complete you discover that the final price shown exceeds the price you were quoted by more than 5%. A deposit can also be reclaimed if a decrease in area or the quality of work on a property will reduce its value by more than 10% or if any of the domestic services proposed are to be omitted. Should this happen, there are formal rules as to how you get back your deposit and it is best to follow these strictly.

The contract usually also states and the conveyance *must* state what guarantees for the completion of the property are being provided. Such guarantees may be 'intrinsic' or 'extrinsic' depending on whether certain circumstances allow the developer himself to give the guarantee or whether he must have recourse to a bank or similar financial institution. Information prior to the signing of any contract regarding these guarantees is a matter of some importance since they provide for the return of deposits and stage payments if the building is never completed.

Indeed very careful early investigation in the case of purchases 'on plan' is becoming more and more important since a fairly novel marketing procedure is sometimes applied to purchases of this kind. On occasions, developers will ask potential buyers to sign *contrats de réservation* either just to test the market or to provide evidence of interest in a development to a possible lender of finance. There seems no harm in this provided that any deposit paid is paid (as in fact

French law requires) to a notary or to a blocked account with the developer's bank. Thus, if the development never gets off the ground, there will be no trouble in getting it repaid. Standard French books on this subject hold that the *contrat de réservation* complying with all the requirements of French law is the *only* valid contract which can be entered into and all others are void. There have been cases where non-French option agreements have been offered as preliminaries to *contrats de réservation* and option payments taken under them. In such cases, the most careful advice should be sought as to the validity of such agreements.

You are entitled to receive a draft of the conveyance a full month before completion and notaries for developers are fairly good about this. If you have instructed someone to advise you in France, do not hold on to these papers when they arrive but send them straight on to them otherwise the time available for investigation will be short.

Note that the *Loi Scrivener* which is the law which deals with house purchase loans referred to in Chapter 4 does not apply to purchases *en l'état futur*. This does not mean to say that you cannot by agreement make the same arrangements in such a sale (that it is conditional to your obtaining a loan within an agreed period) but you have no right to the benefit of this condition as you have in the purchase of an existing property. This is a point which is not likely to cause much of a problem since it is improbable that a developer will not agree to such a condition being inserted in the contract.

What to do on the completion of building

In due course, when the building is completed, you will be asked to make the last stage payment, leaving 5% of the total price unpaid. At that stage, you are asked to inspect the property and confirm that all is in order and, if you find that it is, you hand over the balance of 5%. You are strongly advised to call in an expert to make this inspection for you. It is true that you have a right to call on the developer for a period of two years for small problems and for ten years in the case of major defects to put things right but there are obvious reasons why it is better to have these put right at the outset. A developer will react more positively to an expert's complaints in order to get his final 5% than to yours after he has had all he expects to get.

This is really a case where the services of a surveyor or architect are needed. If you are not satisfied with the work which has been done, try to resist the temptation to put the final 5% on deposit with the seller's notary to be released on completion of the outstanding work. Refusal to do this may lead to you being refused possession of your flat, which can be distressing, but yielding to the wishes of the seller may in the long run prove more distressing. Pass your problem over to your surveyor or architect who is much more likely to be listened to than are you.

All these rules apply specifically to purchases on plan. They are in addition to the general rules on buying property dealt with in Chapter 4.

6 Financing your purchase

About 50% of UK buyers of property in France buy with the aid of a loan. Whilst it must always be sensible to make your borrowing arrangements at an early stage, if you are borrowing in France, because of the special protection given by the French *Loi Scrivener* (page 27), it is not necessary to have a firm offer of a loan before you sign a contract as you would normally do in England. On the other hand, if you are borrowing in England on the security of property in France, the law is not applicable to you and you should have got your loan arrangements tied up before you make the decision to buy.

As you will have realised from the Chapter on The Buying Process, in France you can be pressured to sign a contract within minutes of having seen the property you would like to buy which, of course, is the reason for the protection afforded by the law when it applies. Of course, if the amount of the loan you can raise determines the price you can afford to pay, then you ought to establish as soon as you can the percentage of a purchase price you can borrow which is unlikely to vary much unless you intend buying something very expensive.

It is highly desirable to start off within the right price range for it is very easy to succumb to a property you cannot afford if, as is not infrequently the case, the selling agent is a more expert seller than you are a buyer.

As you have probably found from experience, you need very careful advice when you are borrowing to buy a house in

England: at least you are aware in outline, if not in detail, of the alternatives available and their advantages and disadvantages. When you are thinking of buying in France, not only do you have more alternatives available but many will involve considerations which are new to you. It is essential that you seek the right advice from the right person and as you will see, you may need advice from more than one person.

Background

What is said in this Chapter assumes that you are domiciled and resident for tax purposes in the UK and are likely to remain so. On that basis, it is very unlikely that you need concern yourself with French tax rules about mortgages but the person or company from whom you ask advice should know if you need such information and where you can get it.

Until recently, there were only two usual methods of raising funds to buy a house outside of the UK. You could borrow in the UK on the security of property you owned there, then use the cash to buy a house in France or you could borrow from any of the lending institutions in France itself on the security of your French property. On the whole, UK lenders were not over-anxious to lend on your house in the UK for you to use the loan outside the UK but the upsurge of British interest in the French market and thoughts of 1992 have much changed that attitude.

What is more important is that UK banks and a few building societies are increasingly willing to lend on the security of non-UK property and, in the case of France, some French lending institutions such as Banque Nationale de Paris have opened offices in the UK specifically to help English buyers of French property to raise loans and provide advice on how best to proceed.

Obviously the method you choose must be that which best fits your personal circumstances. The points to consider are discussed below.

Using your French property as security

There has never been much difficulty for the foreign buyer of property in Franch to obtain a loan. On the whole, the criteria are the same as in the UK. Lenders need to know that their borrower can service the loan but they seem to give more significance to the value of the property to be bought than to the ability of the borrower to repay. It is quite rare for a lender to ask for a valuation or have a survey made unless the purchase price is very large, though it is possible that their local expert is in fact consulted.

Lenders will require a first mortgage on the property you are buying. Of course, the legal system and procedure are different from the English system but there is absolutely no need to be afraid on that score provided that you are being properly advised on the effect of French law. In the long run, lenders the world over are the same — if you fail to make repayments, you risk losing your house but otherwise they leave you alone.

If you are borrowing in France from a French lender, the *Loi Scrivener* will apply as between you and that lender. There are very stringent consumer protection rules with a basic ten day cooling-off period after the loan offer has been received. Unlikely though it is that your lender will try to break these rules, always let your adviser see the loan offer before accepting it and *never postdate an acceptance* so that you can go home and the lenders can hold it until the ten day period is up.

It will be a condition of virtually every French loan that you take out insurance with death, sickness and accident cover and against the possibility of your being made redundant during the term of the loan. The premiums are not high. The rule in France, unlike England, is that the borrower is responsible for effecting his own insurance on the property, and the lender will require a certificate of insurance. Every lender in France requires the borrower to effect life cover, which sometimes includes accidents and sickness cover. The premiums are not high and under 50 years of age a medical is usually not required. See the Chapter on Factors to Bear in Mind.

Using your UK property as security

Although you are now on more familiar ground, expert advice is nevertheless needed. After all, it would be unpleasant to lose your French holiday home because you could not keep up the mortgage payments but it would be disastrous to lose your home in the UK because the borrowing or extra borrowing on its security became too much of a burden. On the other hand, many house-owners have untapped equity in their houses which could be used towards the purchase of a house in France or even other assets available as security for a UK loan.

There is no doubt that a far greater range of possibilities and considerably greater flexibility are available from the English mortgage market. France has not got a series of sophisticated options for raising house purchase loans, possibly because the French are not a nation of house-owners (the letting market flourishes) but it seems likely that competition from outside is on its way and France may yet develop at least some of the loan raising options available in the UK.

The variety of loan raising methods which are available in the UK makes it essential that you seek advice on the most suitable option for your purposes. Companies which have a wide experience of all the factors involved should be consulted and all the facts put before them. There are fairly standard rules applied by all UK lenders when considering how much to lend — such and such a percentage of the value of the property, such and such a percentage of the borrower's income and the like. The advice you need is not only how much can you borrow but which is the best way to borrow and that advice is much more skilled than it may seem. This is why the best possible advice from those with the widest lending experience is essential.

Currency considerations

Of the many considerations involved in borrowing for a house purchase in one country when you live in another is the currency in which you should borrow. For those who cannot restrain their gambling instincts or who consider themselves financial wizards, this is a point usually of more significance than to the run of the mill buyer. If you borrow in currency A, you pay interest on that loan and make capital repayments at currency A rates. At the time you take out the loan, they may be much lower than those of currency B. If the loan interest is at a fixed rate, this may give you a significant saving. On the other hand, what happens if the rates of exchange have moved against you when you have to buy currency B in order to make payments to your lender? All you hoped to have saved, is lost in one of a series of exchange variations. You can reduce this risk by arranging to be able to switch the currency of your loan every so often but unless you are a foreign exchange dealer, you risk becoming too ill with worry to get much pleasure out of your home in France.

Of course, it is true that sterling is now linked to a number of other European currencies so that its fluctuations are somewhat limited. It does seem on the face of it undesirable to earn in one currency but be obliged to pay out of those earnings over a period of time in another currency.

Should you borrow in a currency which is not that of the country of your lender? The answer must, be that if you feel you wish to borrow in this way, you must take advice from a highly qualified expert. If you follow the advice he gave you and his prophesies were correct so that you made (or did not lose) money, you may clap your hands. If his advice turned out to be wrong and you lost money, do not blame the expert; blame yourself for ever having thought of taking exchange risks with your holiday home in France.

As this book is at pains to point out, every person who lives in one country and buys property in another asks for — and usually gets — just what he deserves if he does not avail himself of the advice which in fact is always at his service. Few aspects of this kind of buying call more loudly for competant advice than the provision of a loan towards the purchase.

7 Building new property

It is perhaps less easy to find suitable land on which to build a single house in France than in many other Mediterranean countries. This is because in the areas which are most popular with the British either almost all such land has already been bought — very often by developers for building estates — or it is agricultural land or/and designated as not available for building for other reasons under local planning schemes. Of course, there is building land available but it will be considerably easier to find in fairly remote areas where it may be difficult in the future to find a buyer for the house you have built.

Remember that if you wish to sell your property, the buyer may well not be British. Since France is very much larger than the United Kingdom travelling distances are greater. 'Getting away from it all 'assumes for the French reasonable proximity to all those things which the British do not want to see for miles around when they make for their country cottage.

Some general thoughts

It must be a safe rule to follow — in France as elsewhere — that if land which looks very tempting is offered to you as building land in an area where such land is normally hard to come by, there is probably a very good reason why it has not been sold already.

There are still old houses available for restoration which in many cases amounts virtually to rebuilding. From a planning point of view, renovation or additions may well incur the same problems as new building so this chapter applies in large measure to acquisitions for both purposes.

In areas recognised as those where the visitor buys property, it is in the interests of planning authorities to foster building, provided it complies with normal planning exigencies. In other areas, where the tourist is not such a common sight, the French can be less welcoming towards the foreigner.

There is another very important distinction between buying land in or near developed areas and out in the country. French succession law keeps family property in the family and it is not rare to find land in the country owned in small proportions by a large number of members of one family. It can sometimes prove quite difficult to get all the co-owners to agree to sell, either because one or more of them is quite happy to blackmail gently as to the price or because some member of the family thinks it would be disloyal to part with a plot which has been owned by the family for generations. In towns and less remote parts of the country, developers have long ago discovered the technique for overcoming this problem.

Planning

Within the last few years, planning in France has been decentralised and is now dealt with at local level. This means not only that planning applications can be dealt with more speedily but also that a considerable amount of planning information can be obtained from the local *maire* and, in small communities, the *maire* is likely to be the authority on whose decision the outcome of your application depends.

Even if you are fluent in French, it is not wise to try to cope with planning problems yourself; you would never do this if you were building a house in England and, in France, procedure counts for everything. It may well be useful to visit the local *maire* for some basic preliminary information if you have been introduced to a piece of building land or even to ask what *constructible* land in the area exists but, after that, you had best leave it to the experts. A visit to the *maire* at the beginning is a useful public relations exercise in any event.

France also has its listed buildings, *monuments historiques*. As in England, houses which are protected in this way cannot be altered without permission and often cannot even be painted inside or outside except in colours approved by the appropriate authority. If you have in mind restoring a listed building, make very certain what you can and cannot do. The information is often more difficult to obtain than in the UK and it may be dangerous to seek advice only from a local run of the mill architect.

Do-it-yourself planning

However, if you feel that you can cope on your own, the following is some basic information.

Plan d'occupation des sols (POS)

Virtually every local authority area in France has published a planning scheme. As in England, this indicates the permitted uses of all land covered by the plan. Certain small *communes* do not have a published POS and, in these cases, only the most limited building will be permitted in their areas.

Certificate d'urbanisme

This certificate is the equivalent of the answer to a planning enquiry made of an English local authority. The situation as defined by the local POS together with all other planning regulations and density rules affecting any particular piece of land are disclosed in this certificate which is always obtained on every purchase, whether it is of land for building or of an existing house or flat.

Permis de construire

With the exception of a few types of work not likely to be involved in the building of a new house, a *permis de construire* must be obtained before building can begin. The formalities for making an application for this must be strictly followed. Notice of the application is made public so that objections may be raised. In most cases, a decision must be given within two months of lodgement as to whether the application is granted, refused or deferred for a period which may not exceed two years. If no decision is made within this period, the application is deemed to have been granted but since it can be withdrawn during the next two months, it is not safe to rely on an implied grant. Once granted, a *permis de construire* is valid for two years. Building work must begin within this period or the *permis* lapses as it does if work is suspended for more than one year. A *permis* can at the discretion of the authority which granted it be extended for a further year.

Certificat de conformité

On completion of building work such a certificate should be asked for. When granted, it confirms completion of building work in compliance with the *permis de construire* (but not with planning regulations generally). It is a document of great importance and should be carefully retained. The date of the certificate is the start of a three-year period after which the planning authority can take no action if it is found, for example, that the building was not built in conformity with the *permis de construire*. It also marks the beginning of the five-year period during which the building is subject to TVA on sale.

Remember that most purchase contracts are prepared not by the seller's lawyer but by an estate agent very often with nothing more to go on than what the seller tells him. It is, therefore, of the greatest importance when buying building land not to sign anything without taking advice. Any contract you do sign for the purchase of land should be conditional on a *permis de costruire* being granted in the terms asked for. A *certificat d'urbanisme* saying that your land is *constructible*) ie is available for building the kind of house you have in mind) is not sufficient. Also, if applicable, the contract must be conditional on SAFER (a quasi-governmental agricultural committee which oversees on a local basis the use of agricultural land) and possibly on the local authority waiving their rights of compulsory purchase. Unlike the situation in England, the equivalent of local searches are not made before but after exchange of contracts.

Building

From a practical point of view, there are four different methods of getting a new house built. You can:

1 Buy the land with the house to be built on it from a developer using usually (but not necessarily) his plans. This is buying *en l'état futur d'achèvement* or 'on plan'. Special rules designed to protect buyers apply to this method (and also to buying a flat in a block which is still under construction) and are dealt with separately in Chapter 5.
This method has the advantage of allowing you to pay by instalments as building progresses. Whilst you will not be

able to alter your plans radically in midstream, it is usually possible to get the developer to make some changes although these may increase the agreed price.

2 If you already own land, you can get a professional builder to build you a 'one-off' house. He will normally offer a number of basic types but some variations can be made. He will undertake all the professional and technical work, in many cases subcontracting to various trades. Again, the law is strict in order to protect you. You are entitled to insist on a fixed price and to either a guarantee from a bank or similar institution to ensure completion of the work or to pay by instalments only as work progresses. As you will see from the figures quoted below, much, if not all, depends on your choice of builder on which you must get prior advice.

3 Instead of using a professional builder, you can put your trust in an architect of your choice (but not of the estate agent acting for the seller of the land). The architect should be either someone who has proved their worth by working for trustworthy friends of yours or be recommended by a totally independent and qualified person. There are a very few English surveyors and architects working in France but finding one avoids the language problem. If you use a French architect, you must have a bilingual intermediary or you will inevitably have surprises. A recent survey has shown that to make use of an architect increases the overall cost of building (including his fees) by about 12%. Even with an architect watching over progress, the more often you put in an appearance on site the less should be the inevitable delays.

4 Finally, you can (but are not recommended to do so) with or without the help of an architect, make your own arrangements with local building trades. It gives you sole control over what is going on which is almost certainly just what you should not have.

Currently, method 1 is used for about 15% of the new houses built in France, method 2 for about 40%, method 3 for about 35% and method 4 for under 10%. The following figures may also help you to decide how you are going to set about building.

	Table I: Methods of house building				
	Alterations to contracts	*Price revisions*	*Delay in completion*	*Legal action needed*	*Bankruptcy of builder*
Method 1	5%	5%	30%	5%	nil
Method 2 (top 10 firms)	23%	39%	16%	7%	nil
Method 2 (others)	22%	18%	34%	9%	13%
Methods 3 & 4	7%	10%	26%	5%	7%

If you decide to employ an architect and to entrust everything to him, you should discuss with him what you have in mind before you enter into any contract to buy the land. In this way, you should be able to ensure that your contract has all the necessary conditions in it so that if they are not fulfilled, you can 'cry off'.

What not to buy

There is of course land on the market which is unsuitable for building, waiting to be sold to the ill-advised or the unadvised. Among the reasons for land being unsuitable are:

1   there is only a limited supply of water for household use,
2   there are geological problems often well known to the seller but not to you or anyone else not familiar with the area,
3   there are drainage problems,

4   local geographical problems such as sloping ground,
    prevailing winds, frost pockets and fog pockets.

All these matters should be borne in mind at pre-contract
stage. Do not be overconcerned with steep slopes and rocks:
good builders know how to deal with this. It is also a safe
rule to be very suspicious of land for building sold to you by
a builder.

For discussion with your architect

If the piece of land you have in mind fits the bill, remember
also that the climate and way of doing things in France
(particularly in the southern parts) can be very different from
those in England. Among the things useful to discuss with
your architect at an early stage are:

1   the siting of the house. If you are in the south, you will
    probably spend a good deal of time outside. You may be
    yearning for the sun but after a time shade becomes
    important. Terraces and balconies should be placed
    accordingly,
2   discover what the prevailing wind is and take account of
    this when discussing siting,
3   space and how it is used are important for just as it is
    expensive to rectify oversights to a house so it is
    expensive to alter the interior. Is your holiday home going
    to become a permanent home? If so, it is perhaps better
    to have too many rooms in the beginning so as to have
    sufficient accommodation later on,
4   you will probably be required or at least strongly
    encouraged to build in local style. Do not resist this. A
    house which is not built with local materials in local style
    sticks out like a sore thumb,
5   consider very carefully all the methods of heating: gas, oil,
    electricity and solar. In the north of France and well
    down towards the south, you should think more or less in

terms of an English winter. Even in the south, it can be chilly and damp in the winter months,

6 most houses in France have some kind of shutter. They are essential to keep out the heat in summer and the cold in winter,

7 modern French houses and flats do not lack light switches and electric points but they are often very oddly placed. You will have to insist on having yours where you want them. In general terms, the quality of electric fittings, plugs, switches etc leaves much to be desired. Although all modern buildings have circuit breakers rather than fuse boxes, French appliances tend to be un-earthed more often than in the UK. Outside plugs are very useful,

8 work surfaces tend to be lower than in the UK. A height of 92–94 cms is the norm in Britain,

9 if you are in the south and a keen gardener, see if you can have an emergency water tank for use on lawns and plants if and when there is a shortage of water with an automatic watering system,

10 security is important, if not to you, at least to your insurance company. If you have a holiday home which is often left unoccupied, grills over the windows and a strong front door are essential,

11 parts of France become very hot in summer and very cold in winter. Proper insulation is therefore essential. Luckily, France is one of the most advanced countries in the world in this field. There are not only special plasterboards, using glass-fibre and/or polystyrene but also special foam-filled partitions as well as architectural methods of creating internal air pressures to act as insulators. However, to take advantage of all this technology you must discuss the subject with your architect. If you find out too late that either your architect has not allowed for this kind of protection or that the builders have 'skimped' the work, it is very expensive to deal with insulation once the house is built.

This is not an exhaustive list and if you have a good architect, he should think of a lot more points. It does also help to seek advice from your neighbours. Do remember that too much which is out of the ordinary may be unreasonably expensive.

Your building contract is something you must not attempt to agree without specialist advice. This is even more important if the architect is the choice of the builder but, even if he is your choice, get the contract vetted by a lawyer before you sign it. The list of what can go wrong or provide you with surprises because you have failed to take advice is too long to set out here. You deserve all that can happen to you if you sign a building contract 'blind'.

8 You and French banks

Whether you are buying property in France for a permanent or a holiday home, it is almost inevitable that you will need a bank account in France or at least come into contact with the French banking system. It is possible not to have a bank account and to exist on Eurocheques and credit cards but you will soon realise that this is impractical. On the other hand, it is not a good idea to close your UK bank account or to throw away your UK credit cards even if you are living in France permanently. To maintain the former gives you a certain freedom of action and to keep the latter avoids having to use French credit cards which require you to pay off the whole outstanding balance every month by direct debit from your French bank account.

UK branches

On the whole you will benefit from using the French branch of your own bank in the UK. Three of the 'Big Four' have branches in France which provide full banking facilities. Although they are subject to French banking law, they are familiar with English banking procedure and most of the branches will have at least one member of the staff who is English. In many cases, the manager or assistant manager will also be English. This helps from a language point of view because he can talk if necessary to your branch in the UK in terms which they understand and, also, it facilitates the transfer of cash between the two countries.

There is no exchange control in France. However, there are still some limits for large transactions which may not be carried out without Banque de France consent and the movement of more than 50,000 francs in cash (in any currency) over French frontiers should be reported to Customs. However, there are no restrictions on foreigners buying or selling property in France and no difficulties about getting the proceeds of sale of property out of France.

Bank accounts

The formalities for opening an account in France are similar to those in the UK. The bank will need a copy of your passport and a 'fiscal' address. For those living permanentiy in France, this will be in France and for those whose permanent home is out of France, it will be elsewhere. Despite the fact that Exchange Control has gone, there is still a loose description of 'resident' and 'non-resident' given apparently to those who have or have not got *permis de séjour* and cheque books are still marked to show a non-resident account as used to be the case. It seems to have no significance except easily to identify the non-resident to the authorities. On the whole, joint accounts have advantages, if only because on the death of one holder, the other can usually continue to draw.

Both current accounts and various types of deposit account exist. At the moment, interest on deposit accounts owned by by account holders not fiscally domiciled in France is paid free of French withholding tax but this advantage for the UK tax resident may disappear if certain proposed EEC tax rules come into force in France.

You will be supplied with a cheque book, usually within a few weeks of opening an account. You are strongly advised to order a new cheque book at the same time as you receive your first cheque book and continuously to repeat the process. There are some special peculiarities about French bank accounts which it is essential to note.

Rules about cheques

In effect, all cheques are crossed although bearer cheques do exist. Their use, which is very rare, seems to imply to the French and their tax authorities that some kind of tax fraud is involved.

You cannot negotiate a cheque, that is, you cannot get a cheque from someone in your favour and, by signing it on the back, pass it on to a third person. Cheques can only be paid into your own account and then need endorsement as do cheques on which you draw cash for yourself at the bank.

A French cheque cannot be 'stopped' unless it has been stolen or lost and you must report this to the bank. If you stop a cheque for other reasons, the results may be curious and unexpected for the British. This involves very complicated French law and the only proper advice which can be given is that, before you do this, go to see your bank manager or your lawyer.

You cannot give a postdated cheque, that is, you *can* give it but it will be cleared on the day of its presentation whatever the date may be on the cheque.

If words and figures on a cheque do not agree, the words prevail. If a cheque is more than six months old, it will be treated as 'stale' and not cleared. Most branches of British banks would contact you in either case and query the situation, but many branches of French banks would not.

Bank drafts (*chèques de banque*) are not treated as cash as in the UK but are cleared as though they are ordinary cheques. This can be infuriating when you pay in to your branch of the X Bank an English bank draft drawn on the Paris Head Office of the X Bank only to find that you are not given immediate value for it.

Ordinary cheques take longer to clear than in the UK. Bank statements often duplicate themselves in their opening and closing entries. This, coupled with the slowness of clearing cheques means that you have to treat the balances shown on your statements with reserve. It is possible to get photocopies of paid cheques but not to get paid cheques returned with your statement. Sometimes this is necessary as the French are frequently not very good at accounting and will sometimes deny receipt of payment unless you can produce proof of the debit of the cheque. If you do not live permanently in France, make certain that statements are sent to you in the UK and not to your French address.

Special rules apply to 'bouncing' cheques but are too complicated to describe in detail here. Although it has been calculated that about one in every 1,500 cheques 'bounce', the rules are considered sufficiently effective to allow most shops to accept cheques without cheque cards merely on proof of identity. In short, if you issue a cheque which cannot be met, your bank will inform you and you have 15 days in which to put this right. If you fail to do this, your cheque book will be taken from you and you will not be allowed to issue cheques for a year or to operate any other existing account. The fact will be reported to the Banque de France which prevents you from opening any new accounts during that period and violations of this ban are reported to the police. One of the problems of this situation is that it affects an innocent joint holder of an account but equally, it can be remedied if it was caused by a genuine error.

Direct debits

This is what is known as payment by *prélèvement*. It is extremely useful in the case of electricity, gas or telephone bills since it avoids your arriving home only to find no light or telephone. The bank pays the bill but does not check it. You will be sent direct a copy of the account to check. Do not use this method for paying *taxe d'habitation* or *taxe foncière*: It is best to check these first and you are allowed plenty of time in which to pay.

How best to make use of your bank in connection with property purchases is dealt with in Chapter 4.

Property purchase loans

There are a number of French institutions in the property mortgage market. They take the place of the UK Building Societies although they are quite different in concept. Virtually all the banks are also lenders for property purchases. Each institution has its own rules but, in general, it should be possible to borrow up to 75%, or perhaps a little more, for a permanent home, and 50–60% for a holiday home. The length of loans in France is shorter than in the UK and on average 10 to 15 years would be considered normal. An offer of a loan can usually be obtained quite quickly. See Chapter 4 for more details.

In quite a number of cases, where the loan is less than a certain amount or a certain percentage of value, the lender will not have a valuation made, and when an inspection is made of property offered for mortgage, it is generally for valuation rather than for survey purposes. You will not, therefore, be able to find out if there are any defects in the property such as you can in the UK when, for example, a building society will retain part of a loan until certain repairs have been carried out.

Protection of the borrower

There are stringent rules about mortgages for the protection of borrowers. Reference to these is made in Chapter 4 about the effect of these rules on purchase contracts. As between lender and borrower, the most important are:

1   every loan offer must contain full details of the terms of the loan offered and it must remain in force for 30 days,
2   the offer cannot be accepted before the end of a ten-day 'cooling off' period,
3   acceptance of an offer of a loan is subject to the condition that the loan is taken up — and therefore your purchase is completed within four months,
4   the loan offer may forbid early repayment of part of a loan by instalments of less than 10% of the original loan. A penalty may be charged for early repayment but it may not exceed the rate in force from time to time set by the Government,
5   if a borrower makes default and the lender does not call in the loan, he may instead increase the rate of interest within certain permitted limits until the borrower is no longer in default. A borrower may apply to the court for relief if, for example, he loses his job or becomes ill.

If the loan and purchase are dealt with simultaneously, there is only one document, not a separate *acte de vente* (conveyance) and mortgage, and it is preferable for a variety of practical reasons to carry out both transactions together.

9 The French tax system

Whether you are leaving the UK permanently or whether you intend to go on living here but have a holiday home in France, you must get advice from experts who know *both* French and UK tax law. In the case of French tax law, there is a distinct advantage in getting advice in France from a local tax expert rather than from a firm out of the area.

For many years the Double Tax Treaty with France has included an arrangement for the exchange between the two countries of personal tax information. At present, the link between France and the UK in tax matters is not as close as that between France and certain other countries but EC arrangements are intended to remedy this.

The taxes

The following taxes will affect you as a buyer (and on occasions as a seller), or as the owner of a house or flat, in France, irrespective of whether you live there permanently:

1 stamp duties *(enregistrement)* payable on the purchase of property,
2 VAT *(TVA)* on the purchase of building land and on certain sales of houses and flats,
3 annual taxes *(taxe foncière* and *taxe d'habitation)* on the ownership and occupation of property,
4 capital gains tax *(plus-value)* on the sale of property,
5 inheritance tax *(droits de succession)*.

It is very unlikely that you will become subject to French wealth tax *(Impot de solidarité sur la Fortune)*, which is a tax on the value of capital assets payable by persons resident for tax purposes in France in respect of *all* their assets. Non-residents are liable in respect of their assets in France. It is payable by private individuals only and is not payable unless your assets exceed 4,260,000 francs for the year 1991 when the rate is 0.5%. This rises step by step to a rate of 1.5% on a taxable capital in excess of 41,280,000 francs. The threshold tends to rise every year and you must get advice if you think you might be caught by this tax.

Resident or non-resident?

It is unlikely that you will be resident in France for French tax purposes unless you are also the holder of a *carte de séjour*, which confirms your right to live on a permanent basis in France. You can be resident for tax purposes in more than one country but, on the whole, this is not to be recommended. You are liable to pay French income tax (ie you are a French tax resident) if:

1   you have your *foyer* or home in France. This can be where your family lives even if you spend most of your time travelling elsewhere,
2   your principal place of residence is France, which it is deemed to be if you spend a total of more than 183 days in any one year there,
3   you carry on a profession or business activity in France unless it is ancillary to a main activity carried on elsewhere,
4   the centre of your economic interests is in France, ie most of your investments are there or you direct your business activities (which are not in France) from France.

Do not worry that the French tax year starts on 1 January and the UK tax year on 5 April. This can cause problems if your UK income is large enough and you are liable to French tax but they can usually be sorted out if you take advice from your accountant in good time.

Domiciled or not domiciled?

This is a very important question. It affects mainly inheritance tax, both in France and in the UK, and also what is going to happen to everything you own when you die. The answer can also decide if it is useful to make certain kinds of investments. Your domicile is the place where at any moment you intend living for the rest of your life. Often it is safer, though sadder, to consider it as the country in which you would prefer to die. Husbands and wives under English law can have separate domiciles. As a general rule, the English Revenue will fight hard to claim that you have an English domicile if it will bring in inheritance tax. It helps them to prove the fact if you are living abroad by giving away any sign that England is still your home for example, in your Will that you would like to be buried in the plot you have bought somewhere in England.

Advertising your domicile is so important that if really you leave England never to return but always to live in France, you must continue to make this clear all round at every possible opportunity.

French taxes

Enregistrement

Fortunately, the basic rate of stamp duty on the purchase of land is virtually never exacted, for it works out at about 17%. There is a wide variety of exceptions of which you are likely to meet the following:

1   on the purchase of all 'new' property (ie within five years of completion of construction) from the developer himself, and on the first sale within that period, the rate is nil but small Land Registry fees are payable on the ex-TVA price,
2   on other purchases of property to be used as a private dwelling house the rate is about 7%–8%,
3   on building land the rate is nil and no Land Registry fees are payable,
4   there are various reduced rates of duty applicable to land used for agricultural and other special purposes.

It is important to note that:

1   when 'new' property is being sold, it is often incorrectly advertised as being sold with *'frais de notaire réduits'*. However, it is the stamp duty only which is 'reduced'; notarial fees are unaltered,
2   the rates quoted above are approximate. This is because stamp duties consist of departmental and local duties which vary slightly from place to place plus an overall percentage on the duty thus arrived at,
3   in certain cases, in order to obtain a reduced rate of stamp duty, you have to undertake to use the land or house for residential purposes within a limited period of time. Failure to do this will result in the full rate being charged plus a penalty,
4   where you have a house with land, an area of 2,500 or sometimes 5,000 square metres goes with the house for stamp duty purposes. The remainder of the land will be charged at a higher or possibly full rate.

French VAT (Taxe sur la valeur ajoutée — TVA)

When you buy land for building, you will pay TVA, currently at 13%. So, when a purchase price is quoted to you, you must usually add on this tax to calculate the total cost (no stamp duty is payable).

TVA will be payable on work done to build your house and the current rate is 18.6%. It is more usual in France for prices or estimates to be quoted ex-TVA *(hors taxes)* rather than TTC or *toutes taxes comprises.* (See also capital gains tax.)

When you buy 'new property', you will be quoted a price which includes TVA. The amount of this tax will be shown separately in the conveyance to you and the seller will account for it to the tax authorities. If you sell within a five-year period of completion of the property, you will be liable for TVA on the sale price and you will quote a TVA-inclusive price to your buyer. You will be liable for the TVA on the sale price less the TVA already paid on the purchase price, adjusted to take account of any changes in the rate. So, unless you sell at a considerable profit quite soon after you have bought, your TVA liability will not be large.

Annual taxes on property

These are *taxe foncière* and *taxe d'habitation.* The former is payable by the owner of property, usually quite a small amount and is calculated on notional letting values. *Taxe d'habitation* is also calculated on this basis and is payable by the occupier, whether owner or not. This tax is the equivalent of general rates in the UK and is payable to the local authority or *commune.*

Ownership and occupation are established as at 1 January in each year. Therefore, if you buy and take occupation of property on 2nd January, you will probably get a tax-free year. In theory, *taxe foncière* is apportionable between seller and buyer but this rarely happens; *taxe d'habitation* is not apportionable.

Taxe foncière is not payable during the first two years after completion of a new property. There are a number of circumstances resulting in reductions of both this and *taxe d'habitation* and it is worth while making enquiries to see if you qualify.

These and other taxes should not be paid with English cheques as this may cause problems for the local authorities. You are allowed approximately two months in which to pay and thereafter there is a 10% penalty.

Income tax

You are not liable to pay income tax simply because you have bought property in France. Indeed, you could become liable to pay French income tax without owning any property in France, although this is very unlikely. The calculation of income tax in France is as complicated as in the UK and the rates and reliefs change just as often. If you do become liable to French income tax, you can obtain help from the local tax office or from a local accountant. However, if you have any large or unusual non-French income, you should seek professional advice.

Capital gains tax

Basically, every person non-resident in France for tax purposes is liable to capital gains tax (CGT) on any capital gain made on a sale of French property. The basic rate is 33⅓% of the taxable gain. This tax is dealt with more fully in Chapter 19 where you will find when you are exempt from this tax and what happens if you are not. Non-residents are also liable for CGT at 50% on sales of assets other than land.

If you are tax-resident in France, the odds are that the house you live in will be your principle private residence and therefore, as in the UK, exempt from tax. If it is not exempt on that basis, there are a number of rules which mitigate the liability in certain cases.

Inheritance tax

Droits de succession differ radically from the English counterpart in three respects:

1 it is not payable out of the estate at a rate which is linked to the value of the assets of the person who has died,
2 the rate at which it is paid depends on the relationship of the beneficiary to the person who has died and each beneficiary is liable for his own tax,
3 there is no surviving spouse exemption.

Wherever you are domiciled and/or resident, inheritance tax will be payable on all your assets in France. If you are domiciled in France, which almost certainly means that you are also resident there for tax purposes, this tax is also payable on all your assets outside France, wherever they may be. The value of your estate will be calculated on one of these bases and divided amongst your beneficiaries who will each pay their appropriate tax. However, as in the UK, it is a tax which is related solely to the death of a person and his assets, and its payment does not depend on whether or not a beneficiary who pays the tax is resident in France.

The rates of tax operate on a 'slice' basis. When the beneficiary is a spouse, child or parent, the rate starts at 5% on assets not exceeding 50,000 francs, progressing in stages to 20% on assets between 100,000 and 3,400,000 francs and on again in stages to 40% for assets in excess of 11,200,000 francs. In the case of brothers and sisters, the rates are 35% up to 150,000 francs and 45% on the balance. More distant relations pay 55% and non-relatives pay 60%.

There are a number of reliefs of which the most important currently, are:

1 in the case of spouses, children and parents, no tax is payable on the first 275,000 francs,
2 in certain circumstances, brothers or sisters, who in any event must have lived with the person who has died for at least five years before their death, do not pay tax on the first 100,000 francs,
3 physically or mentally handicapped beneficiaries do not pay tax on the first 300,000 francs of what they inherit,

4   any beneficiary who does not benefit from any other reduction does not pay tax on the first 10,000 francs,
5   beneficiaries with three or more children get a reduction per child on the tax calculated as above,
6   It is intended that from 1 January 1992 (the date has no EC connection) surviving spouses will pay no tax on the first 330,000 francs of their inheritance and parents and children will be allowed the first 300,000 francs free of *droits de succession*. In addition, these allowances and the allowances of 100,000 francs for aged or ill brothers and sisters will be cumulative with that of 300,000 francs for beneficiaries who are handicapped which was not previously the case.

Interest is payable on *droits de succession* from six months after the date of death of a person who dies in France and 12 months if they died outside France. Arrangements can be made for the tax to be paid by instalments or deferred in circumstances similar to those in force in the UK.

The tax on gifts *(droits de donation)* is calculated in the same manner as *droits de succession* by reference to the amount of the gift and the relationship between the maker of the gift and the receiver. However, depending on the age of the giver, there is a percentage reduction: the younger the giver, the greater is the reduction.

The impact of French inheritance tax, the manner in which it is assessed and the persons on whom it falls, coupled with French succession rules (see Chapter 16), make it essential, if you intend to acquire property in France, to take the most competent advice and to plan your investments accordingly. The terms of your Will and whether you should have a French Will and an English Will, or one only, are points of vital importance and are discussed in detail in Chapter 17.

Offshore companies

For some years, the French tax authorities have been aware
that the use of non-French companies as owners of land in
their country can lead to the reduction of French tax. Until a
recent convention on the subject is ratified by France, trusts
are unknown to French law. The successful use of a non-
French company for this purpose involves a considerable
amount of expert knowledge and no one should ever indulge
in an exercise of this kind without it. Never take the advice
of a friend who says he has avoided French tax in this way
and remember that if you make a mistake it may cost a 3%
tax on the *capital* value of your house or flat in France every
year and the conveyance to the company will carry stamp
duty at the *full* rate of not far short of 20%.

10 Time-sharing

If you have had an enjoyable holiday in France, you may feel that you would like to spend many more holidays there. Of course, you can stay in a hotel but this is not the same as being in your own home. You can also rent a flat or house but it is very disappointing when, having enjoyed yourself there, you want to rent it again next year only to find that it is fully booked. Alternatively, you can buy a flat or a house but you may feel that it is expensive just to use it for two or three weeks a year.

If you have family who can use your own home in France in your absence or if you think that you would not mind letting it during the time when you cannot be there yourself, buying a flat or house may be the answer even if you can be there yourself for only a few weeks every year. But if neither of these ways of reducing the cost of owning a home in France attracts you, the answer may be time-sharing.

Avoiding problems

France is not a country which sets out to attract the foreign buyer in preference to the French buyer so that since the French are unlikely to fall for the 'get rich quick' methods of the sellers of time-shares in other countries, you will benefit from their attitude. Naturally, there are exceptions to this because you may have to buy not from the original owner of a property divided into time-shares but from someone who has owned the time-share for some time and is trying to sell it to you in England. If you follow the advice given below, you should avoid most of the problems.

The French Government has tried to protect people from the misleading technical terms used to describe time-sharing. By the use of the word *propriété* (ownership) linked to other words which have no meaning in French law, sellers of time-shares implied that the buyer was getting full ownership of a flat. In addition, although the concept of time-sharing is simple enough, it was not covered by the legal system.

The costs of time-sharing

As the word implies, time-sharing means that instead of buying a flat outright, you buy the right to occupy it for a specified period in each year. In France, time-sharing is almost exclusively limited to flats but it can also apply to houses.

The period in the year during which you can occupy the flat and the number of occasions in a year when you can exercise that right set the price you pay. For example, if the flat is in an area where the holiday season is in summer, July and August will cost more than January or February. If it is in a ski resort, the winter months will be more expensive than the summer months.

In some cases, you may be able to exchange your time-share period for a period in another flat either in France or elsewhere. You will almost always be able to allow someone else to occupy the flat during your time-share period and it will be very rare to find any restrictions on selling it.

In addition to paying the price of your time-share, you will be required to contribute to the overall cost of managing the block which contains the flat you occupy. The method of calculating this is explained later in this chapter.

This chapter assumes that your time-sharing block was built or adapted so that the original seller of the time-sharing periods was a single person, or a company owning the whole block. The management of the block, the amount of control you have over the quality of the management, and its cost to you, depend on which method is used to set up the time-sharing scheme. Sometimes, you will find that one person owns two or three flats, not the whole block, and then sets up a time-sharing scheme just for those flats. This may cause problems and it is best to avoid buying a time-share in these circumstances.

Some general guidelines

The Office of Fair Trading in London has issued guidelines for those buying a time-share outside the UK. Because of recent changes in the French law on time-sharing, these now contain good advice in connection with the purchase of almost any kind of property and do not apply specifically to French time-shares. Remember:

1   never to sign any contract or document under pressure or without having it explained to you by a lawyer who knows both French and English law. It is very unlikely that your solicitor in England himself will be able to advise you unless he has had a number of years' practical experience in France,

2   to ask carefully about maintenance costs and expect that they will be underestimated. Some amenities may not be originally provided but will subsequently become necessary and their cost will probably fall not on the seller but on the time-sharers,

3   to make certain that you have someone in France who can look after your interests,

4 to make sure you know exactly what it is you are buying, that you can afford it and, above all, never think of buying a time-share as an investment.

Old system *v* new system

There are now two different legal systems in France for time-sharing. Under the old system, you bought the right to occupy a flat for a given period of time between given dates. This right was not 'land' as a lease is 'land' so that it could not be registered anywhere. It was merely a contract between you and (usually) the owner of the block allowing you on a personal basis to occupy the flat in exchange for which you paid a lump sum and then an annual sum to cover your maintenance charges. The original owner (or possibly someone else he designated) was responsible for maintaining the block, cleaning your flat before you arrived and after you left. From a practical point of view, if the flat was badly managed, there was little you could do and, in general, the time-sharer was at the mercy of the maintenance set-up against which there was no simple method of enforcing complaints. As to the amount of service charges, these were extremely difficult to check and almost impossible to control.

The new system which came into force in 1986 makes use of a type of French company which owns the whole block housing the time-share flats. You buy not a time-share but shares in the company, which give you the right to occupy a particular flat during a designated period. The main points to note are that:

1 this modern method is not obligatory. However, prospective time-sharers are well-advised to try to find a block where it is being used. For some time to come, this may mean that it will be desirable to buy time-shares in a new building rather than from an existing time-share owner,

2   the type of company used (a *société civile d'attribution*) is really no more than a partnership but when this is used for a time-sharing scheme it gives the shareholders the same protection as though they were shareholders in a UK limited company,

3   all decisions relating to all aspects of the time-sharing scheme are taken by the shareholders at company meetings. In this way, the time-sharers are masters of their own destiny provided they are sensible enough to exercise their rights.

Most company decisions are by simple majority and shareholders (ie the time-sharers) may and should appoint proxies unless they are certain of being able to attend meetings and are fairly fluent in French.

The shareholders appoint (and can dismiss) a managing agent who manages the block, pays bills, negotiates contracts, employs staff etc and, of course, is accountable to the shareholders. The annual service charge is fixed on the basis of these accounts after approval by the time-sharers at a company meeting.

The way in which a time-share block is managed under this new system is much the same as for a condominium (see Chapter 11). In both cases, your presence at meetings personally or by a proxy is necessary. It is inevitable in the case of a time-share company that a considerable number of shareholders must be absent from their flats when meetings are held and you may find it useful to make use of MPOA to vote on your behalf (see Chapter 11). Company meetings are not usually held in English even if the majority of shareholders are British and all correspondence will be in French.

Ownership of a time-share period through the ownership of shares is safer than under the old system. The new system allows time-sharers to take part in their own management and the ownership of the shares which allow you to occupy your time-share flat is a matter of record. Under the old system, the contract was a private one between you and the owner of the block only and was of no value as between one time-sharer and another or indeed anyone else. Your right to occupy a flat under the old system and your shares in the time-sharing company under the newer system can pass under your Will in English law.

There are special rules about the documents to be used when buying (or afterwards transferring) shares in a time-sharing company: they tell you everything you need to know about the company and about your rights. If you are buying under the old system, there is no obligation to provide any kind of information but it is essential that you demand as much as you can. In any case, whether under the old or the new system do not try to be your own lawyer: use your local legal expert and through him, under the new scheme, the services of a *notaire*.

If you buy under the old system, all you will receive is a contract which sets out rights and liabilities and the transaction cannot be registered anywhere.

If you buy under the new system, you will receive a copy of the Articles of Association *(Statuts)* of the company of which you are a shareholder. These will set out the rules for the management of the company and the time-sharing scheme and will show the flat and the period(s) of occupation allotted to you by the shares you have bought. It is not customary for French companies of this kind to issue share certificates. You can prove your ownership of your shares by the confirmation of the managing agent and every transfer of shares must be notified to, and approved by, the company.

In France, a fairly new and rather unusual form of time-sharing *(bi-propriété)* exists which divides the year into two parts and only two owners are involved. This produces an interest in land which can be registered at the French Land Registry. It is a mixture of ordinary joint ownership and time-sharing and, if it is offered to you, it is important to seek advice.

11 Life in a condominium

Since French law requires that any building, parts of which are owned by different people, must be treated as a *copropriété*, or condominium, it is certain that if you buy a flat in France you will buy it *en copropriété*. There will also be occasions when you buy a house, or land on which you build a house, on a building estate *(lotissement)* where the *copropriété* will play an important part in your life. Although your house will be your own individual property, the parts of the estate which are used by all the house owners, such as the access roads, possibly the gardens of each house and all the amenities on the estate — the swimming-pool and the tennis-courts — will be owned jointly by the house owners.

Costs of flat ownership

The French have more experience than the British of living in flats and of sharing the cost of maintaining a block. Various methods of sharing costs have been tried; the current method, which dates from 1965, is to divide the cost of managing a block roughly according to the value of each flat based on a number of factors. However, as this calculation is often made before the block is built, there is little point in using your percentage share of the service charges as a guide to the current value of your flat.

The system of *copropriété* is unknown in England and it would be a great pity if it were allowed to take over from the existing English system of buying a flat by taking a long lease from the owner of the block or by taking over the lease from an existing flat owner. However, one advantage of the French system is that the rules and regulations which govern the management of a French condominium must abide by the Law passed in 1965 (as from time to time amended) so that neither developers nor the flat owners themselves can make rules which are unreasonably restrictive or unfair.

Systems of flat ownership

There are several basic differences between the French and the English systems. In England, the usual system is for each flat owner to own his own flat but not to have interest in the common parts of the block: the roof, the staircases, the drains etc. In France, you own your flat but, in addition, you have a share in all the common parts of the block, including the surrounding land, swimming-pool etc.

Under an English long lease of a flat, you have many obligations to your landlord; your landlord probably has many less towards you but they will include maintaining the block in exchange for which you pay a service charge. In France, you have no landlord. You have a similar list of obligations and the liability to pay a service charge which are contained in a document called *règlement de copropriété* but your obligations are towards your co-flat owners. In England, therefore, you have a number of flat owners on the one hand, often represented by a Tenants' Association, and a landlord (or possibly a management company) on the other. In France, every flat owner has obligations towards every other flat owner.

In France, everything to do with a condominium, its rules, its management and the part you are expected to play in it, is in French, this is part of 'living abroad'.

Finally, you must get used to the fact that the ownership of a flat in France is neither freehold nor leasehold. This need not cause you any problems and you are free to sell it, let it, mortgage it, give it away or leave it by Will. The easiest way to treat it is as a freehold which has no land attached to it.

Obligations and liabilities

Before you complete the purchase of a flat, you should get a copy of the *règlement de copropriété*, which sets out your obligations and liabilities as a flat owner. You should ask for a copy of this from an existing owner before you sign a contract to buy and from the developer of a new block before you sign any contract with him. Although it is desirable to see this document as early as possible, as most of them are drawn up by notaries and either incorporate or refer to the Law of 1965 (with some recent amendments), it is not a disaster if you cannot. If, however, you are buying a flat in a building built before 1965, you should make more persistent enquiries.

This is because either you will have a *règlement de copropriété* which was drawn up before that date and so must be read as amended by current Laws or because there is no such document and the co-owners must rely entirely on those Laws for information. There is just a possibility that if there has been no sale of a flat for a very long time, the method of ownership of the flat is not direct but through the ownership of shares in a company which gives the right to the occupation of the flat (see Chapter 10 on time-sharing for a modern use of this method). This method of owning flats is now seldom come across and all that need be said is that if it should apply to a flat you are buying, you will need special explanations from your adviser.

When you manage to obtain a *règlement de copropriété*, which is often combined with a *cahier des charges* and sometimes

loosely called by either name, you will find that it contains
the division of the block into *lots,* giving each lot its share or
quote-part in the communal areas of the block. *Quote-parts*
are usually expressed as fractions of 1,000 or 10,000. The
document will also contain:

1   the share of service charges attributed to each *lot,*
2   rules about the calculation and payment of service
    charges,
3   a list of what each flat owner may and may not do,
4   rules applying to the management of the block,
5   rules applying to meetings of flat owners,
6   a variety of rules dealing with certain eventualities, such
    as if the block is burnt down, if additions to the block are
    made or if it is desired to join two flats together, etc.

Service charges

These may be divided into general and special charges.
General charges will apply to expenses common to all flats;
special charges are those applicable to individual blocks in a
complex or, more unusually, to a flat or group of flats which
enjoy an amenity which the others do not. Usually, general
charges will be the same proportion of the total general
management expenses as your *quote-part* and, in most cases,
the proportion of service charges payable by a flat is
unalterable.

Service charges are based on an annual budget presented to
the Annual General Meeting of the flat owners. It is
customary to collect these charges in advance by two, three
or four instalments each year, depending on how much cash
in hand is needed at any one time, and the final instalment in
every year is a 'topping up' payment. Sometimes an
additional payment is asked for either to cover a special item
of expenditure or to ensure that there is always something in
the management 'kitty' or *fonds de roulement.* Failure to pay
service charges will result in the payment of interest and
ultimately legal action. Service charge accounts are not always

easy to follow but the *syndic*, or managing agent, should be
able to explain them to you.

What you may and what you may not do

In general, you may make alterations to the inside of your
flat provided that you do not interfere with any of the
common parts of the building. You would be wise to discuss
any major alteration with the *syndic* (see below) in case what
you have in mind requires consent. You must be careful with
balconies and terraces which might seem to be part of your
flat but which are in fact a common part of the building.
This prevents you, for example, from repainting your terrace
yourself.

You will certainly be required to conform to the standard
type and pattern of exterior blinds and urged not to dry
clothes on your balconies. Domestic animals are normally
permitted but parking your car, except in designated parking
spaces, is forbidden.

You will be required to insure your own flat in respect of
certain risks and usually to produce a certificate of insurance
to the *syndic* (see Chapter 13 for insurance of property).
Overall insurance of the block is the responsibility of the
condominium as a whole and forms part of your service
charge.

You must use your flat only in accordance with the purposes
permitted in the *règlement de copropriété* and this will
normally be as a private dwelling house. However, mixed,
private and professional users are common in France and, if
you want to practise as a doctor, dentist or architect etc from
a flat, you will probably be allowed to do so.

Management of the block

The flat owners as a group form a *syndicat* and appoint a

syndic to manage the property, normally on a one-year basis. The *syndic* is responsible to the condominium for its day-to-day management and may be helped in this by a *conseil syndical* or executive committee, the members of which are flat owners who are appointed annually. The *conseil* will normally check the *syndic's* annual accounts as it is rare for outside accountants to be employed. Since it is almost essential to have a *syndic* available from the start of a new development, and there are at that time no flat owners available to appoint one, it is usual for the developers to appoint the first *syndic* for subsequent approval by the flat owners. Unfortunately, flat owners seldom 'unappoint' him in time.

A good *syndic* makes for a happy block. A bad *syndic* is a disaster. There is very little fellow-feeling among flat owners unless two or three band together. There is, however, a simple rule for extracting the maximum pleasure out of your flat from a management point of view and getting things done — be on excellent terms with your *gardienne*. Listen to all her woes, make her small presents and avoid some of the less harmonious things that your fellow flat owners can do in a block of flats.

Meetings

This is the moment when flat owners can have their say. Certain unalterable rules apply to meetings:

1 there must be at least one General Meeting each year to approve accounts and the *syndic's* management for the past year, to pass the next year's budget, to (re-)appoint the *syndic* for the next year and to deal with any other items on the agenda,
2 additional meetings can be called by the *syndic* and can be requisitioned by flat owners but the proportion of flat owners needed to do this is sufficiently large to ensure that this rarely happens,
3 fifteen days' notice of meetings must be given either by

registered AR post or by delivery by hand. Flat owners may, not later than six days before the date of the meeting, ask for additional matters to be put on the agenda but it is almost inevitable that British owners who receive notices in the UK will be unable to exercise this right.

Flat owners may attend meetings either in person or they may give a proxy to someone else to attend in their place. A proxy may act for up to three flat owners or for more than three flat owners provided that the total number for which he acts as a proxy does not give him more than 5% of the votes. Most condominiums allow anyone, whether he is a flat owner or not, to act as proxy but it is permitted to restrict him to a co-owner. Neither the *syndic* nor any member of his family may act as a proxy.

Most matters are settled by a simple majority of votes. Certain resolutions, such as the dismissal of a *syndic* or alterations to the building, need larger majorities and some may need the consent of all the flat owners. In parts of France where flats are largely owned by absentee owners, it is quite common for there not to be a quorum present at a meeting. In this case, a further meeting will be called by written notice and the people present at that meeting, in person or by proxy, will count as a quorum. However, this does not apply to the resolutions which need a 100% agreement of all flat owners.

Meetings are usually chaired by a president who is a member of the *conseil syndical* and the secretary is frequently the *syndic*. Scrutineers are appointed to count votes and the meetings are conducted in French.

Minutes of all meetings must be prepared and circulated amongst all the flat owners. Minutes can vary considerably in quality but should show who presided at the meeting, and should list those who were present, those who were absent, and the resolutions on the agenda and whether they were passed.

Members absent from meetings

There is no requirement that any of the documents or proceedings of a French condominium should be in any language other than French. Unless you are reasonably fluent in French and able to be present at all meetings of a condominium you should appoint a permanent proxy who conveniently could be your legal adviser in France. You might think it worthwhile to appoint as a permanent proxy an organisation such as Mediterranean Property Owners Association, which undertakes this task for an annual fee and reports and advises on what takes place at such meetings.

12 Renting property

A large proportion of the population in France lives in rented accommodation. The French tried a measure of rent control early in the 1980s and soon discovered that it became very difficult to find flats to rent. After about five years, rent control more or less disappeared and flats for rent re-appeared. In July 1989, many of the previous rules were re-introduced and rent control and the protection of tenants will presumably come and go according to the policies of successive governments.

The ideal way to find a permanent home in France is to choose the area where you want to live and then to rent a flat for six months whilst you are taking a careful look around. Leases must usually be granted for a minimum of three years, but tenants are required to give only three months' notice (or in certain circumstances less) to quit. On the death of a tenant, the lease passes to the surviving spouse and/or children and certain other persons living on the premises for at least a year prior to his death.

As is usually the case with leases, most of the burden falls on the tenant. Apart from paying the rent, the tenant must insure the premises, keep the interior in a reasonable state of repair and behave 'in a suitable manner'.

As in England, a three-year lease of a flat is likely to be a standard document since most of its contents are laid down by law. Lawyers are not usually involved in leases of this type. If you are taking a lease from a reputable firm of estate agents, whilst often there may be little to worry about, it is always safer to have it 'vetted' by your local legal expert.

Points to note

1   You will be amazed at what a French landlord asks for in the way of references. Apart from rent receipts for many years past, which you will not be able to give if you own your house in England, he may ask for income tax receipts and bank statements. If you use a branch of a 'British' bank in France, ask the manager to phone the landlord's agents and to speak in your favour. It is unlikely that you will ever miss a lease because you cannot provide what is asked for and you can usually come to some sort of compromise.

2   A lease must be in writing. It is illegal for the tenant to be asked to pay more than one-half of the landlord's agents' commission.

3   The fixing of the rent which may be charged is quite complex and may ultimately be a matter for the court. You must make careful enquiries to be sure you are not overcharged. If the lease contains a rent revision clause it can only take effect once each year and the revision must be linked to the Cost of Construction Index.

4   It is highly desirable, but not obligatory, to have prepared an *état des lieux* (schedule of condition) when you move into the premises. Make sure that this is prepared meticulously. Your landlord will insist on another *état des lieux* (schedule of dilapidations) being taken on your departure and this is why it is so necessary to have the two schedules available for comparison.

5   If you do not pay rent in advance at intervals of more than two months, you may be required to pay a deposit, which may not exceed two months' rent which may not be used for unpaid rent during the term of the lease. When you leave, the deposit must be returned to you within two months of your quitting the premises less any amount you may owe the landlord for dilapidations. Reputable firms of agents will see that your deposit is returned within the proper time but this is, alas, by no

means always the case. If you have had trouble with your landlord's agents or if you are dealing direct with your landlord, it is worthwhile thinking about not paying your last two month's rent and letting the deposit answer for it. You are not *advised* to do this but it is a fairly standard practice.

6   You will pay in addition a small annual stamp duty on leases.

Repairs

It is inevitable that the flat you rent will be in a condominium. The repairs of all the common parts of the building, for which you as a tenant are not liable, are the liability of the condominium as a whole. That same liability will, as between you and the landlord, be his liability and his alone. This is the cause of many problems. For example, if your flat is on the top floor and the roof starts to leak, only the *syndic* of the condominium can repair it but he has no duty towards you to do so. As far as you are concerned, it is your landlord who is liable to get the roof repaired but he is not allowed to do it himself. If you complain to your landlord, he will ask you to complain to the *syndic*. There is no way of avoiding this but it stresses the need to rent a flat only in a block which is in a good state of repair.

Insurance

Because of the landlord's liability for repairs, make sure that you are fully insured for contents and other internal risks. Your lease will require you to insure against 'tenant's risks', which is a type of comprehensive cover for the interior of the flat and for damage which the flat might do to others, for example, if the bath water overflows. You are free to choose your insurance company; the landlord cannot compel you to use a particular company.

Service charges

The law states which items in the service charges a landlord may pass on to a tenant. Normally, you will be asked to make payments on account with your rent and, once a year, you will be supplied with extracts from the landlord's service charges accounts, when you will be asked to pay the balance. You cannot attend meetings of the flat owners but you can insist upon evidence from your landlord in support of his demands.

Since it is so easy to extricate yourself from a lease, leases cannot be assigned without your landlord's consent, which he is not obliged to give. Subletting is permitted with the consent of the landlord, who is entitled to know what rent you are charging the subtenant.

Tenants are protected in possession. Private individuals must grant three year leases and company landlords leases lasting six years. If the landlord does not give notice to quit at the end of the lease, it is automatically renewed for the same period. A landlord may, however, offer a new lease on other terms provided they comply with the law.

If a landlord has special professional or personal reasons which are stated in the lease to retake possession within the three year period (but not in the first year), he may do so. However, he must give two months notice and if the event he is relying on does not happen, he cannot rely on it later. In order to obtain possession at the end of a lease, the landlord must either prove he has 'legitimate and serious' reasons for so doing or that he wishes to live in the premises himself. He may also give notice if he wishes to sell, the tenant then has a two month option to buy at the open market price, if he refuses and the landlord sells to another at a lower price, the tenant may (if he ever finds out) require the sale to him at that price. There are special rules for the protection of elderly tenants.

13 Settling in

Assume that you have bought your property and have chosen it to suit your future intentions. It may be just a holiday home or it may be that you have decided to live in France on a permanent basis. Or it may be that it is a holiday home which will become your permanent home on retirement. As discussed in Chapter 9, it is very unlikely that you will become liable to French income tax unless you have your permanent home in France. However, if you obtain the necessary permission to reside permanently in France, you will become liable and will have to make the appropriate arrangements.

Applying for permanent residence

Because you are a citizen of an EC country you automatically have certain rights to reside and to work in every other EC country. In practice, this freedom is limited to some extent because most countries like to keep a check on the entry of foreigners even if they come from another EC country. You need formal permission to reside in France on a permanent basis. However, as a British citizen, you may stay in the country for three months at a time without any formalities.

Visa de longue durée

If you intend to take up residence permanently in France, you must apply to one of the French Consulates in the UK for a *visa de longue durée*. This involves completing a form and providing evidence that:

1 you have somewhere to live in France,
2 you have an income sufficient to keep you from being a burden on the French State,
3 you have a medical certificate.

Proof of a home in France can either be a copy of the lease or conveyance to you of your home, or you can ask the notary who dealt with the purchase to give you an *attestation d'acquisition* to prove the purchase. On the whole, the *attestation* is more useful as you will probably need it again for the import of your furniture; it is one sheet in length and photocopies are accepted. The average *acte de vente* may be at least 20-pages long and is often not available until several months after you have completed your purchase.

Carte de séjour

It takes about six weeks to obtain a *visa de longue durée*. You need to take this (it is stamped in your passport) to your local *bureau des étrangers* in France and, in exchange, you will be given a receipt entitling you to a *carte de séjour* which is initially valid for one year.

This is the procedure which any French Consulate in England will advise you to follow. In fact, it may be possible to short-circuit the procedure depending on where you are intending to live. The *préfet* of each *département* in France is authorised to grant *cartes de séjour* directly to EC citizens without the production of a *visa de longue durée*. There is no list showing which *préfet* will exercise his discretion to do this and so you must make enquiries in the area where you will be living.

Your 'papers'

Generally, the French have a very relaxed attitude towards 'papers'. French identity cards are not obligatory (although a Frenchman without one would be highly suspect) and you are not required to carry any other form of identification. However, to avoid complications with the CRS (or riot police) it is useful to have your *carte de séjour* available and this also serves as identification when you make payments by cheque.

When any kind of identity document is needed, you must obtain at least three passport-size photographs of yourself. Remember that *timbres fiscaux*, with which you pay for the document you want, are obtainable at some tobacconists but never at a post office.

Your car

As soon as you have a *carte de séjour* you must apply for a French driving licence and if your car has British plates you must re-register it. Normally, you will be given back your UK licence once all the details have been taken from it but the French do check with Swansea.

Making the move

Few people are likely to buy furnished property in France and it is advisable not to do so. You must, therefore, decide whether to export your own furniture from the UK or to buy afresh in France. If you are making a permanent move, you will probably prefer to take your own things with you. In many cases, this will be a sensible decision because many items are more expensive in France and some, such as carpets, curtains and silverwear are, in general, of a lower quality. However, if you are going to live in one of the hotter parts of France your furniture will probably be unsuitable: on the Mediterranean coast, where you can live out of doors for six months of the year, the hot sunshine and the salt atmosphere of the sea ruins antique or good-quality furniture.

Importing furniture can be relatively relaxed providing the correct procedure is followed. Hiccups can occur, however, as a result of the inconsistency of operating this procedure through different regions of France. The interpretation at the port can be somewhat different to that of a local office in the south, for example, and the paperwork can be horrendous.

It is worth remembering also that you will not be allowed to sell any duty-free imported furniture in France for ten years.

Importing duty-free goods

The rules governing the import of duty and tax-free household goods to furnish a home in France are simple and generous. Provided that you have owned the goods for at least three months and have paid VAT on them in the UK (antiques are free in any case) you may freely import all your personal belongings, furniture and furnishings, either in one consignment or over a period of 12 months, for use in your new permanent home. All that is needed is an inventory (in French) in duplicate and a copy of a lease or the *attestation d'acquisition* to prove you have a home in France. The procedure is slightly different for the furnishing of a holiday home, when you are limited to items reasonably needed for this type of a home. In this case, you must send an inventory (in French) in triplicate to the Regional Director of Customs in the area where your holiday home is and, in due course, you will receive back the necessary authority.

A basic knowledge of French should suffice for the inventory: there is absolutely no need to spend money on using a translation service. Remember that your television will be useless in France if it is not dual standard because the French use the SECAM system. Otherwise, all electrical equipment used in the UK can be used in France although you should check microwave ovens some of which are electrically suitable only for the country in which they are sold.

These rules are based on procedures used in all EC countries so they should not vary. It is, however, as well to check them at the time you want to make use of them. It is not safe to rely either on French Consulates or removal firms; the safest thing to do if you are not in France yourself is to ask a friend in France to obtain the latest Customs leaflet.

Using a removal firm

Although the French Customs procedures are very simple, it is worth while using a firm with international experience to move your goods to France. You may be surprised at how expensive such a move can be and it is advisable to get several estimates. If you do not have too much furniture, try to arrange a part load so that you are sharing the cost with someone else.

In theory, it is possible to do the removal job yourself. In practice, French Customs will deal only with a *transitaire* or customs agent who will, for a fee, arrange the formalities on your behalf.

Insurance

It is standard procedure for most removal firms not to accept liability for loss or damage to your goods in transit. It is advisable to arrange insurance yourself against every possible misfortune that could overtake your goods. There is no problem about values, which should be realistic for insurance purposes, since whatever these may be, duties are not normally payable in France. If you are tempted to do your own removal, you may find that insurance companies are unwilling to insure your belongings.

14 Factors to bear in mind

Whatever you may buy in France — flat or house, new or old — there are a number of points which need special thought.

Utilities

Having moved in, one of the most important aspects of daily life is to understand how to pay for, and therefore ensure continuity of, essential services.

Water

There is absolutely no problem with water in France: it is safe to drink, although the French often prefer to drink bottled water. In general, the water is hard in France with the possible exception of Brittany, Normandy, parts of south-west France and around Grenoble.

It is not the quality of the water which is a problem but that, in certain parts of France which are liable to drought, you may find if you are living in the country that the supply is turned off occasionally. This happens in the UK as well but sufficiently rarely for you not to consider installing a storage tank as a matter of course. It pays in France to make enquiries about this and have a tank of about 1,000 litres for household purposes and, if you are a keen gardener and are allowed to do so, another tank of some 20,000 litres. If your supply is not mains, it is worth while testing it for purity from time to time or installing a filter, but the occasions when this would be necessary will be extremely rare.

What is much more important if you are buying a country property is to make absolutely sure before you buy that you have an undoubted source of water which belongs to you and cannot be turned off by your neighbour or drained away by surrounding owners. Much country property depends on local wells for water and it is often difficult to establish from the title deeds who owns them and who has the right to share them.

Virtually all water not from private supplies comes from the local *compagnie des eaux* which is sometimes owned by the local authority and sometimes is privately owned. Such water is metered and usually paid for half-yearly. When you build a new house yourself, you must get the meter installed by the local water company which charges you for this work.

Electricity

The voltage in France is 220 with the usual tolerance. Wiring is supposed to be in accordance with EC rules but frequently is not, although the green/yellow earth wire is fairly universal. Electricité de France (EDF) is the sole supplier and normally will provide a supply even in the depths of the country although this could be expensive if you are the only consumer in the area. When you install electricity for the first time in a new property which you yourself have built or had built for you, you must produce a *certificat de conformité* to prove that the wiring is up to standard. On a change of ownership, EDF may check the wiring if it is an old house but frequently they do not.

Bills are rendered every two months, alternatively estimated and actual. Payment of their accounts can be done in various ways. If you do not want to pay by direct debit, you can arrange to pay monthly but, unless you are living permanently in France, direct debit is the only method of payment which will ensure that you do not arrive at your French home only to find neither light nor heating.

Figure 3: Electricity or gas bill

Key

1 Address and phone numbers of electricity/gas company
2 Date of bill
3 Total amount of bill
4 Last date for payment
5 Meter readings and consumption in kwh
6 Details of electricity/gas consumed
7 Calculation of TVA and local tax
8 Total amount of bill

Gas

Except in towns, you must expect not to have mains gas.
Where you do, you will find the system very much as for
electricity: you will only be given a supply if your own piping
is in order and you will be charged in the same way as for
electricity.

Where you do not have a supply of town gas (and this
includes not only villages and deep country but also houses
and flats in towns where the builders have not provided gas)
you must rely on bottled gas and this is a common practice.
This will affect your insurance premium. In the case of
country properties, if you are using gas only to cook, a bottle
of gas will suffice and will last an average family for about six
weeks. Remember always to have a spare bottle. If your hot
water system and/or central heating system is also by gas,
you will need a gas tank. These tanks are subject to very
strict safety regulations and can be sited only in certain places
on a property. This is best left to the suppliers of your gas to
deal with. In many cases, you will get a free installation in
exchange for using a chosen supplier's gas.

Telephone

The French have a fairly efficient telephone system although
the lack of an operator can be frustrating as there is no one
available to provide general help. However, there is Minitel, a
small computer which will provide you with phone numbers
and a vast amount of information and which is supplied free
or at very little cost by France Télécom. It is impossible to
describe briefly all that can be done with a Minitel; it is a
must for all telephone subscribers, whether they live in France
permanently or not. To make full use of all its facilities takes
time and an understanding of both the language of the country
and the way in which French programmers think.

There is usually little delay in obtaining a phone except
perhaps in very remote areas. This has to be done by a visit
to your local *Agence Commerciale*. The general rule is that you

must prove your ownership of your house or flat by production of an *attestation d'acquisition* or if you are renting, by showing your lease. Passport or *carte de séjour* will also be required. Sometimes you can get away without these formalities. Phone 14 to speak to your local *Agence Commerciale* in advance to ascertain their requirements. As soon as a line is available, you will get a letter confirming the number you have been given and that you have a *ligne mixte*. This is not a shared line but a line which will take both incoming and outgoing calls. If there is a waiting list for phones and you need one urgently — if you are an invalid, for example — a doctor's letter or similar support will give you priority.

Phone bills come every two months and can be paid by direct debit from your bank or by cash at a post office or *Agence Commerciale* or by cheque to a local area office. If you think it unlikely that you will be overcharged, it is best to pay by *prélèvement* or by direct debit. If you want a receipt for the payment, you must pay with cash.

Be careful about the use of phones you have bought yourself. France Télécom offers quite a wide variety but if you care for none of these, try to buy a phone which is *agrée* or approved. Other varieties can land you in trouble as can cordless phones which are 'tolerated'. On the whole, phones, fax machines, etc not bought in France may be difficult to get repaired.

Figure 4: Telephone bill

Key

1   Date of account
2   Dates of two-month rental period (payable in advance)
3   Cost of unit (which varies according to place called and time of call)
4   Number of units recorded during period covered by account
5   Period covered by account
6   Number of account (there are six per year)
7   Details of special items to be debited or credited
8   Address and phone number of local Manager's office
9   Amount of two months' rent payable
10 Total cost of calls automatically registered
11 Special services
12 Special reductions in cost of special services
13 Total of account and last date for payment

A detailed list of all calls is available for a small additional monthly charge if the subscriber is on an 'electronic' exchange

Figure 5: Detailed telephone bill

Key

1   Number called of which for secrecy reasons the last four figures are not shown
2   Indication of foreign country or *département* or telephone area called
3   Indication of application of a reduced rate
4   Subscriber's phone number
5   Number of telephone account
6   Cost of call
7   Total cost of calls not shown on detailed list
8   Total amount of all calls carried to main account

Television

France uses a different system from the UK so unless you have a dual-standard set, it is pointless taking your set to France.

Sewage

If you are in the country, it is very probable that your house or block of flats will be connected not to main drainage but to a septic tank. Rules about these differ very much from those in the UK and their construction is strictly regulated. If you have your own private septic tank, make certain that you know how often it needs emptying and where you go to have this done. If you are building your own house, make certain that the septic tank is placed where it can be reached easily and that you know exactly where it is.

Running costs and maintenance

When considering the cost of property in France do not forget that once you have paid for the property, you will be involved in annual running costs. These may include:

1   standing charges for electricity, gas, telephone, etc which have to be paid whether or not you are using the property,
2   local taxes if you are only a tenant but both these and property tax if you are an owner and occupier,
3   service charges, if you live in a condominium (see Chapter 11),
4   insurance premiums on both your property and its contents.

At the time you think of buying, it should be possible to assess the total of all these liabilities but to predict what they will be in a few years' time is far more difficult. Remember that a seller of property, and even more so his agent, is liable to quote figures for outgoings at the lower end of the scale and, if you cannot get independent advice on this, add on 20% to the figures you are given for safety.

If you live in a flat, the cost of maintaining your block and its surrounds will be included in your service charge, but you will also want to maintain the interior. If you live in a house, both exterior and interior are your direct concern. Property prices vary widely within France and, where property is expensive, workmen tend to be expensive so that you must also expect considerable price variations when it comes to maintenance.

Insurance

This is a particularly difficult problem. What you are looking for with any insurance company is one which:

1   speaks your language so that you can understand its policies. This will not be found in France unless you happen to buy in an area where there are a lot of British owners and even then there will be problems about explaining to you the differences between English and French policies,

2   will deal kindly but fairly with you when you have a claim and on the whole assume that you are not making false claims,

3   is one from which you can easily separate yourself if you think it has not behaved properly. This cannot be done in the same way as in the UK because you cannot, except in special circumstances such as on a sale of a property, cancel policies at will. Merely not to pay a renewal premium does not result in the policy lapsing; it carries on and you remain liable for the premium unless you have given the necessary amount of notice to the

insurance company that you do not wish to renew. This notice now, as a result of EC directives, cannot exceed two months but this does not absolve you from the need to read very carefully your policy and know what this period of notice may be. Companies will hold you religiously to their requirements and all notices cancelling policies should be sent by registered AR post.

At present, (with one exception) whether you insure your property and its contents through a French or a British company, you will get a French policy. There are British companies which will readily insure French properties and their contents but they do this through their French offices or agencies. Even if you have dealt only with the company in the UK and therefore think you are getting an English policy, you will get a French policy.

In addition, where contents and jewellery are concerned, there are valuation difficulties if any of the items have been bought in the UK, as French and English values differ considerably. The answer to this is to take out insurance with Lloyd's, either in England through a Lloyd's broker or in France through a Lloyd's recognised agent, and they will issue English policies subject to English law.

Whoever you insure with will take into account any period during which your home is left unoccupied and, generally, if you are absent for more than three months in any one year, your premium will be considerably increased. You may also find that during the time you are away, you will not get certain covers, although some companies will maintain these covers if you pay more premium. In certain parts of France, such as the Côte d'Azur, premiums are higher because there are increased risks of burglary not by professional thieves but by amateurs or even tourists.

Making a claim

If you do have to make a claim as the result of any criminal
activity it is necessary to support any claim by a *certificat de
perte* from the police showing that you have reported the
matter to them. Not to report a break-in to the police is
considered evidence that it never occurred. If you have to
make a claim for any non-criminal damage of any
importance, it is worth while considering whether to ask a
hussier (similar to a bailiff) to make a *constat* or report. Such
constats are treated as gospel so that the insurance company
cannot deny what has happened.

15 Health and health insurance

It is a false economy not to take out health insurance when you go abroad. A large number of British insurance companies offer policies to cover everything you might need if you fall ill or have an accident when you are on holiday. Your travel agent will organise a policy for you or, if you are making your own travel arrangements, ask your insurance broker to do it for you. Make certain that the policy covers you for repatriation to the UK if this becomes necessary. If you already have a private health policy, you may find that it will cover you on holiday but you must make enquiries about the extent of this cover. You will probably find that it is available only for a number of weeks per year and there may be special rules if you travel out of western Europe; check also the repatriation situation.

You should also insure your baggage when you travel as a protection against airlines losing your baggage or against thieves breaking into your car.

Reciprocal medical care

You can rely on the EC reciprocal medical care arrangements alone when you go to France, by obtaining a Form E111 before you leave the UK. However, you would not be sensible to rely on this only. The system works well provided you are happy to be treated in a *hopital conventioné*, which is similar to a National Health hospital in the UK. Often such a hospital will admit you and treat you without cost on the basis of a Form 111 alone but sometimes you are asked to pay in advance leaving you to recover your payment once you have returned to Britain. In some cases, it is necessary to contact the DSS Overseas Branch in Newcastle to ask for a Form 112 to be sent to you, which is what the French call a *prise en charge*. This form allows you to have treatment without payment.

You can also get treatment from doctors but you will almost certainly have to pay a fee. You can usually claim this back later but the proportion you receive will depend on whether you have consulted a doctor wholly within the French NHS or one who is in the scheme but who is permitted to charge higher fees. Before you leave home, it is also worth while making enquiries about the International Association for Medical Assistance to Travellers (IAMAT), which provides English-speaking doctors in many of the large towns in France who charge reduced fees. Its European office is at 57, Voirets, Grand Lancy, Geneva, Switzerland. Local Consuls will also provide the names of suitable doctors and hospitals.

You will have no difficulty in finding chemists in France. At least in the larger towns, you should be able to get the medicines you are used to at home although they may be sold under another name. It is sensible, however, to take your own supply of drugs from the UK if you are on a special course of treatment. Chemists in France are closed on Monday morning but there is always one 'duty' chemist (*pharmacie de garde*) in every town open then and also in the evenings and at weekends.

Medical provision for residents

The French National Health Scheme (*Sécurité Sociale*) is available to UK nationals who become resident in France in three circumstances:

1 if you are working in France, you will be obliged, just as anyone working in the UK is obliged, to join the French NHS. The contribution you will pay will depend on your income. However, since the French scheme does not normally pay 100% of your medical bills, you will be advised and probably compelled to join a *mutuelle* (there is one for virtually every type of job in France) which will pay the balance of the cost of medicines and treatment,

2 if you are living in France but not working, you may join the NHS and a *mutuelle* if you wish. Your contribution will be based on your income which means that you have to submit a copy of your last tax return or be assessed at the highest rate which is over 60,000 francs a year. In this case, you would normally be well-advised to take out private medical insurance in the UK (see below) and rely on it alone,

3 if you are living in France and have reached retirement age, you will be in receipt of a UK retirement pension and so you (and your spouse) will be entitled to the medical benefits of the French NHS free of all contributions. All you need to do is to obtain from the DSS in Newcastle a Form E121 and present this to the *Relations Internationales* department of *Sécurité Sociale* in your area and you will be registered and issued with a card and a number. Of course, if you go to France before you reach retirement age and keep up your DSS contributions or have sufficient contributions to give you a retirement pension, you will be sent automatically a Form E121 at the right time. If you were in the French scheme before, and paying contributions, these will now cease.

Sécurité Sociale

Very briefly, the French system works as follows. All visits to the doctor, items bought from a chemist and treatments such as X-rays, blood tests etc are recorded on a brown-and-white sheet of paper called a *feuille de soins*. In the case of treatment, it is signed by the doctor or other person giving the treatment. In the case of medicines, the chemist detaches a label (*vignette*) from the container and attaches it to your *feuille de soins*. In the case of a doctor, you pay him and send off your *feuille de soins* (having kept a photocopy) to your local *Sécurité Sociale* and you will receive reimbursement of the appropriate amount. This varies according to the treatment and the status of the doctor but certain illnesses (heart problems, cancer, diabetes etc) rank for 100% reimbursement. In the case of the chemist, you pay the non-reimbursable proportion and the chemist collects the rest direct. If you are entitled to reimbursement of the payment you have made from a *mutuelle*, the chemist may also deal with this for you but there is no general rule about this.

Medical insurance

There are now many companies in the UK which will give you medical insurance when you are resident in France. Indeed, you may already have this cover in the UK and most companies will allow you to change to an international scheme. On the whole, you will probably do better if you stay with the company which covered you in the UK but there are a number of very important points to consider before you decide whether to stay with your existing company or to choose a new company:

1 will it restrict your travel abroad?
2 will it recover repatriation costs (presumably to the UK) in cases of major illness or death?
3 what exclusions are there for illnesses you have had?

4 are there any illnesses and/or treatments not covered?
5 what level of hospital costs are covered?
6 will it cover nursing at home costs?
7 will it cover other members of your family?
8 is there an age limit for joining the scheme?
9 is there an age limit for provision of benefits?
10 will the premium increase when you reach a certain age?
11 is there a qualification period before the end of which you cannot claim benefits?

Take careful note of the terms on which you can get out-patient treatment under such a policy. In many cases, you may find that it is too expensive to be worth while and the best thing to do is to rely on *Sécurité Sociale* for visits to your GP and for the cost of medicines.

It is becoming increasingly common to find in France blocks of flats specifically catering for the elderly. They exist more or less all over France but it seems unlikely that the English senior citizen will want to live anywhere where warmth and sunshine are not the order of the day. These flats can be bought or leased. There is also a system under which the buyer buys a lease and (in effect) the rent is put towards the purchase of the 'freehold'.

In addition to the normal services provided in a condominium (see Chapter 11), most blocks have restaurants and public rooms where flat-owners can receive guests. Medical services are also provided but these can often be fairly sketchy and not provide more than a simple first aid nursing. There is also the language problem since if one is ill, precise communication with the doctor is essential. At least one doctor in the south is trying to create a multi-lingual set-up to provide medical services to flat-owners in blocks of this kind and at least one English property company which provides accommodation for senior citizens in the UK is thinking of building in France.

On the whole, purchase prices are not much higher than for ordinary flats but the service charges are noticeably higher.

However, for those who either come to France on their retirement or for those who are younger but feel that when they reach that age they would like to know that facilities of this kind exist, flats *pour troisième age* may prove interesting.

Provision for death

In France, all cemeteries currently in use belong to local authorities and the cost of funerals is high. However, the general arrangements are the same as in the UK. Funerals for people of various faiths do not present problems. It is best to leave all the arrangements to the undertakers but to make certain that these arrangements correspond with your wishes and not with what the undertakers think that the typical French family wants. French death certificates do not show the cause of death and this may lead to problems if the body is sent back to the UK. There are no problems about cremation except that there are not many crematoria in France and you are free to choose whether you leave your body or any organ for scientific research. You may find it useful to get in touch with SOS-HELP, which is staffed by English speakers in the Paris region (phone number (1) 47.23.80.80) to help you cope with the difficulties of a death in a foreign country.

16 French succession law

'Unlimited tins of cat food and . . . your children's larder
empty'

This quotation from *Living in France* gives a correct
description of what you may do in your Will in England if
you own only English property. If you prefer your cat to
your children, you can leave all your estate to your cat and
nothing to your children. True, your children can go to court
and in certain circumstances they may get something of what
otherwise would go to the cat, but the fact remains that in
England, you are free to dispose of your estate as you wish.
In France you are not. Certain members of your family such
as parents and children (but not spouses except fairly
minimally in the case of an intestacy) have an absolute right
to inherit certain parts of your assets.

To make things simple, assume that you are a Frenchman
with a wife and a child. You would have to leave one-half of
all you own to that child. If you had two children, the
proportion would be two-thirds and if you had three or more
children, it rises to three-quarters. You would be free to deal
with the remaining balance as you wished and may or may
not as you wish leave it to your widow. There are ways of
'cutting in' a spouse to childrens' shares but only for his or
her lifetime after which the children get all that they are
entitled to.

As you might expect, if you decide to live permanently in
France you will be subject to this rule. However, you might
be surprised to know that the rule applies to your French

holiday home, even if your permanent home is in England and you spend only a few weeks in France every year. This is because, no matter who the owner is, since the land is in France, it is subject to French law.

However, this need not keep you from buying property in France, because if things are properly organised, there is no reason why you should not quite simply avoid the rule.

Avoiding the rule

It is possible to get round French succession rules if you are buying property jointly. When you bought your house in England, you probably bought it jointly with your husband or wife. Your solicitor will have explained to you that there are two ways of owning property jointly. One is that on your death the house passes automatically to the survivor (in English 'joint tenancy', in French '*en tontine*') and the other is that each of you own a part of the house which you can deal with separately (in English 'tenancy in common', in French '*en indivision*'.) You probably chose the former method and your solicitor would probably have been very surprised if you had chosen the other method.

In France, the same two ways of jointly owning property exist, though for quite different reasons. The French almost always use the *en indivision* method for the very reason which makes it usually disastrous for the English to do so: it does not avoid the normal French succession rules. The English should (subject to advice) always buy *en tontine* which is how they would buy in the UK and the property will pass automatically to the survivor.

It is quite impossible to say how many English husbands and wives who have not been properly advised on this point are horrified to learn that they have made the wrong choice. In fact, usually they have not made a choice at all but have signed papers prepared by a notary who assumes that English law is the same as French law and that all English couples buy jointly in the same way as French couples. Usually, it is far too late to do anything about it except at great cost. If you are buying jointly, get advice from a lawyer who knows English and French law and who, if the circumstances require, will ensure that the notary does the right thing.

It is worthwhile giving an example so that you may see how important this is. Remember also that if you are not prepared for it, the problem will arise just at the moment when one is least able to cope with it ie on the death of a husband or wife. Take the following situation, which is not unusual.

EXAMPLE

Mr and Mrs A are married. They have one child. Each has been previously married. Mr A has two children by his previous marriage and they now live with their mother who has remarried. Mrs A had one child by her previous marriage who lives with Mr and Mrs A. Some of the children are under 18 and some are older. Mr and Mrs A have bought a holiday home in France for 750,000 francs. They have bought it by the standard French method of joint ownership (*en indivision*). Mr A dies. Mrs A owns one-half of the house as her own property. Three-quarters of Mr A's half share is divided among his three children (by his existing and previous marriage) and one-quarter goes, if his Will says so, to Mrs A. At best, therefore, Mrs A has five eighths of the house and her joint owners now include children whom she may never have known and with those of whom are under 18 she can come to no arrangement.

It is true that arrangements can be made so that Mrs A can be given a life interest in her husband's share so that she would own one-half outright and one-half she can use for as long as she lives. This is, however, hardly a situation Mrs A wants to learn of for the first time on the death of her husband. She may well have assumed that because her husband's Will in England leaves everything he has to her, she now owns the whole of the house. She is mistaken, however, because French law overrides that Will.

If Mr and Mrs A had bought *en tontine* none of this would have happened. On the death of one of them, their holiday home would automatically have passed to the survivor.

It is true that this method of joint ownership may involve the payment of French inheritance tax whereas the other method might avoid it. Usually, the amounts involved are only a small price to pay to avoid the confusion caused by the imposition of the French law of succession.

There are notaries and others who say that there are dangers in using the *tontine* method because children who have been 'cut out' can claim to be 'cut in'. Take courage from some recent cases on this point which say that it is almost impossible for children to succeed if care is taken and the documentation is correctly prepared. This applies to any Power of Attorney given by the buyer and to the *acte de vente* itself. It is worth taking the right advice to ensure that this happens.

There are at least two other methods of circumventing the succession rules. Only the most competent advice can establish if either may be suitable for you. As a general rule, unless your family circumstances warrant it or you are trying to get out of a very difficult succession situation into which you have been put through lack of advice on a purchase, neither of these methods should be indulged in for properties worth less than three to four million francs.

17 Making a French Will

There are still a lot of people who never make a Will. Perhaps they think that making a Will is tempting fate or perhaps they think that the formalities are complicated; often they cannot make up their minds who to appoint as executors. In most countries, and certainly in England and in France, the way in which your property will be distributed if you die without leaving a Will (this is called 'dying intestate') is based on what it is assumed that you would have stated in a Will but often this is far from what you really wanted to happen.

Therefore, this is a good enough reason for making a Will in any country. But if you are going to live in France, there are special reasons not only for making a Will but also for being properly advised about whether you should make an English and a French Will or whether one or the other will do.

How many Wills?

Try to find a lawyer who is expert in both English and French law to advise you on how many Wills to make. If you cannot find one, go to your own solicitor in England, tell him what you intend to do and instruct him to get some help on French law. Here are some rough guidelines:

1   You are French domiciled, ie you have left England for France with the intention of remaining there for the rest

of your life. In this case, what happens to everything you own, wherever it is in the world, will be in accordance with French law. If all your assets are in France, you need make only a French Will. If you have some assets in France and some in England, ideally you should make a French Will dealing with French assets and an English Will in respect of your English assets, but your English Will will have to follow French law.

2   You are English domiciled, ie you are merely buying a house or flat in France as a holiday home but will continue to live in England, as your permanent home. In this case, what will happen on your death to your house or flat in France will be according to French law, but English law will deal with everything else you own even if, for example, you have cash in a French bank or you own a French car. Ideally, the advice is the same. You should make a French Will covering French assets and an English Will covering English assets. Your English Will, if you have one Will only, however, deals with the house or flat in accordance with French law but everything else according to English law.

Why 'ideally' two Wills?

There is, in fact, no absolute need to have two Wills but in the end it will save your family a lot of time and money. The reason is that England and France have two quite different systems to deal with 'proving' Wills and it is simply not practical to try to deal with one Will in two countries at the same time.

The *réserve*

This is what the French call that part of your estate which must go to certain close members of your family (see Chapter

16). It is a complicated and, for the English, an unusual situation. It need not put you off in any way but you must get advice about it both before you buy property in France and before you make any Will either in France or in England. One more warning: the French have a transaction called *Donation entre époux* or 'gift between spouses'. This is one of the methods of 'cutting in' a surviving spouse, by giving him or her a life interest in your estate in priority to children or parents. You can do this by Will or as a 'gift' whilst you are alive. It simply does not solve the problem of children's entrenched inheritance rights but notaries, unused to English law, suggest that it does. If you and your spouse have been ill-advised so as not to buy your home jointly by the method which will ensure that all will pass to the survivor, you will need advice anyway. At that stage, if all that can be done is to 'cut in' the survivor, you do this by Will — never by *Donation entre époux*. For the British, this is a snare and a delusion and *does not* achieve what you think it does and you should seek professional advice about it.

Types of French Wills

As in England, it is not obligatory to use a lawyer to make a Will in France but, as in England, you would be sensible to do so. The lawyer who advises the French on Wills is the notary. There are three types of French Wills:

The holograph Will   This Will must be entirely in your own handwriting and signed and dated by you. It must not, like an English Will, have any witnesses or any handwriting on it other than yours. Of course, a notary or other suitable lawyer can prepare a draft and you can copy it in your own handwriting.

The authentic or notarial Will   This Will is dictated by you to a notary and your signature is then witnessed by two notaries, or by one notary and two other witnesses.

The secret or mystic Will This is a Will written for or by
the person making it, who then signs it and places it in an
envelope in the presence of two witnesses and gives it to a
notary. The envelope is then inscribed by the notary to the
effect that it is your Will.

In most cases, a holograph Will is sufficient but you must be
careful where you keep it. Do not forget that it is not
witnessed, so there is no one to prove that you ever made it.
Do not put it in your French bank or your family may have
trouble getting it out after your death. It is best left with a
notary or other lawyer who knows you, in France or in
England.

French law allows anyone who is not French to make a Will
in a form which is valid according to the law of his own
country and in any language he wishes. So, you may make a
'French' Will in English form with two witnesses and in
English *but the contents in so far as they relate to the property
subject to French law must be in accordance with French law*.
On the whole, do not try to arrange this by yourself. Home-
made Wills are usually a headache in your own language but
when they have to be translated into French, they can
become doubly a lawyer's joy.

Executors

French *exécuteurs testamentaires* are very different from
English executors. In effect, there is nothing equivalent to
the English executor in French law. Such powers as they
have are supervisory only and last only for a year and a day
from the date of death. They do not administer the estate
which in England vests in them and has to be distributed by
them in accordance with the terms of the Will. It is possible
to vest ownership of assets other than land in *exécuteurs* for
the limited period mentioned above so that they can collect in
and sell or distribute such assets but so far as English owners

of property in France are concerned, they need not be and should not normally be appointed. Your family is, for practical purposes, in the hands of the notary they choose to deal with your estate. If ever advice was needed in the choice of notary, here is an essential time. On the whole, solicitors in England give priority to dealing with estates, but in France, they tend to have other priorities.

Inheritance tax

Inheritance tax declarations (*déclarations de succession*) are made in France usually jointly by all the people who are beneficiaries. Assets tend to be blocked until a receipt for paid tax can be produced so there is an advantage in dealing with formalities as soon as possible. No interest on inheritance tax is payable until six months after a death in France or twelve months if the death took place outside France. In certain circumstances which are very similar to those in England, payment of the tax can be made by instalments or deferred. The delays which do occur in France on a death can cause problems if there is property to be sold. Contracts to sell land can be entered into at an early stage, though it is not very satisfactory to do this. No sale can of course be completed until the land has been vested in the beneficiary entitled to it under the Will and this cannot happen until they have paid the inheritance tax. In fact, it is normally possible to take all these steps together so that the tax is paid out of the sale proceeds but this needs a bit of organising.

Details of liability to inheritance tax are given in Chapter 9.

Final words of advice

If you have both an English and a French Will, you must make certain that they do not overlap. You must also make certain that if you want English assets to pay French inheritance tax, your solicitor includes the correct wording in your English Will.

If you have retained any contact with England, and particularly if you have both an English and a French Will, you must make certain that your solicitor and your legal adviser in France are both aware of what you have done. This is essential because of the different methods of charging inheritance tax in each country. In England, apart from the fact that there is no tax as between husband and wife, inheritance tax is calculated on the value of your assets less your debts and generally paid out of your assets as your executors think best.

Not only is it sensible to have one or more Wills as may be necessary but you must also keep these documents up to date as your circumstances change. An out-of-date Will can be as unsatisfactory as no Will at all, though even that may be better than a home-made attempt.

18 Letting your property

France has reintroduced a measure of control over several types of letting. The two categories which could affect you are holiday lettings and non-holiday lettings.

Holiday lettings

Lettings of this kind are free of all control but they must be genuine holiday lettings. This means that the letting must be:

1 to a tenant who has a permanent home of his own elsewhere,
2 for a period which is clearly within 'the season',
3 of property in a holiday area.

It follows that if you have a flat in a part of France where there is skiing, a holiday letting will be during the winter months and possibly also during the high summer for most of these areas have two seasons. If you want to make a holiday letting on the Mediterranean coast, you could do so in summer and also around Christmas or Carnival time, and if you were letting in Paris, presumably August would be the ideal month.

No one can be a 'holiday' tenant if they have no other home or if they use the premises for business. It is unlikely that tenants from outside France are there except on holiday but you must make sure that this is the case. Obviously, holiday lettings will be for short periods but the test is not the length of the letting period but the length of the holiday season where the letting takes place.

The reason for taking care in this way is that if you discover your tenant is not in fact a 'holiday' tenant, you may have difficulty in ending the tenancy since the letting may be one protected by law.

Rules of letting property

There are certain golden rules about the letting of your own home. You must never assume that anyone will behave in your flat as you would expect to behave yourself. You can try to find your own tenants. This probably means advertising in suitable newspapers or possibly by word of mouth although friends and acquaintances might be able to help. The ideal situation is to build up a list of tenants who return year after year and pass your name on to their friends.

It is wise to take a handsome deposit in advance to cover damages, electricity and phone bills and always to take rent in advance. Your rents will be liable to French income tax but, if you are not resident for tax purposes in France, it is likely that the total rent collected each year will be below the amount at which you start being liable for tax. If you plan to use a French estate agent, you should follow these guidelines:

1 only use a firm which has a good personal recommendation from someone whose judgement you trust,
2 difficult though it may be, if you have views about the nationalities of your tenants, you must tell your agents,
3 you should not be charged more than about 15% commission and you should agree this with the agents at the beginning,
4 most agents use a standard tenancy agreement but, for

very short lets, no agreement is worth much. What is essential is that the agreement states the tenant's home address and that they are using your property only for holidays,

5   there are some agents who retain deposit cheques and do not pay them in until the end of the tenancy or return them if they are not needed. This is absolutely improper. All rent and deposit cheques received by agents must be banked as soon as they are received,

6   experience and enquiry will help you to decide on the proper rent for any given period. Agents may let the property for more than you expect, then keep the balance and charge both you and the tenant commission. It is worth checking with tenants the amount of rent they were paying.

Whether you let through an agent or organise lettings yourself, you must not forget to arrange for each 'turn round'. Some agents will deal with this but others will not. It is not always easy to find someone you can trust to do this for you after each tenant leaves and before the new one arrives. In some blocks, the *gardienne* will do this for you but as most 'turn rounds' happen on Saturday afternoons or on Sundays, she may not be prepared to do this.

However good your agent may be and whatever promises have been made to you, it is foolish to expect a regular income from holiday lettings. Ideally, rents from short lettings pay for your own holidays or your outgoings for the rest of the year. You should buy property in France either for your own holidays or for a permanent home, and not because it is in a good letting area.

Long-term lettings

If you are going to be away from your home for a long time, you can let it, but you must be aware of both the law which governs the circumstances in which you can regain possession and the various other factors which affect your relationship with your tenant. There are often restrictions on the amount of rent you can charge and there are many technical requirements which you have to fulfil.

This does not mean that you should be discouraged from a long-term let. Many more people live in rented accommodation in France than in the UK and you should have no difficulty in finding a tenant. As usual, the question is, is he or she the right tenant? As bank references in France are not normally obtainable, it is acceptable for a landlord to ask a prospective tenant for their last six rent receipts and even their tax returns. The most sensible thing to do is to put yourself in the hands of a reputable firm of agents who will organise the letting for you. Lawyers are not usually involved in drawing up leases of private dwellings. Although agents will be able to complete the blanks of a standard form of lease, you must make certain before signing anything that you have understood your rights and liabilities. If you have any doubts, your local legal adviser who helped you buy the property should be able to explain everything to you.

General guidelines for letting property

1 If you are letting a flat in a condominium you are free to do so provided that your tenant behaves properly. If you are contemplating a long let, it is advisable and sometimes obligatory to inform the *syndic* and you should always tell the *gardienne* if anyone other than yourself is occupying the flat: friend, relation or tenant.

2 Whether the letting is a holiday let or a long-term let, you

must make sure that your tenant is aware of the rules in the *règlement de copropriété* of the condominium.

3   On a long let, you will be able to pass on to your tenant some of the service charges. You can do this by agreeing a round figure to be added to each rent payment and then once a year giving to the tenant a copy of your service charge account to check and asking for a 'topping up' figure if necessary.

4   Do not forget to check your insurance position. You should certainly inform the insurance company of your lettings.

5   If you have a series of short lettings, make certain that each tenant complies with the internal regulations about car parking, use of the swimming-pool or other facilities and not hanging up clothes on the balcony to dry.

Chapter 12 looks at the situation more from the tenant's point of view, but it should be read in conjunction with this chapter if you are thinking of letting your property.

19 Selling your property

It is impossible to know when you buy a property how long you are going to remain in it or what will be the reasons for wanting to sell it. No one other than the expert should buy property in France purely as an investment but that does not mean to say that you should not expect its value to keep pace with inflation.

Sale price

There is no doubt that a well-cared-for flat or house sells more easily than one which is dilapidated but you must remember that furnishing styles vary enormously from country to country. However, in general, it is advantageous to include the furnishings in the sale price. Second-hand furniture and equipment of any kind commands only the lowest possible prices in France if sold separately from a home. Therefore, it is preferable, if you do not need them elsewhere, to add something on to the sale price for kitchen equipment, such as dishwashers and refrigerators, rather than to try to sell it elsewhere.

If you have bought a 'new' flat, so that the stamp duty you paid was well below the usual rate, and you were the first buyer from the developer, and you sell within five years of completion of the building, your buyer will again pay a low stamp duty. With the high rates of stamp duty in France, you may think that this makes the flat cheaper and easier to sell, but this is often untrue. Since high stamp duties are payable on 'old' properties, their sale price reflects this.

Alternatively, the price of a 'new' property may be increased to take account of the low stamp duties.

Estate agents

Take the greatest care in your choice of estate agent as their quality can vary widely. It is preferable to choose one who is well recommended by an *independent* source. Remember that French agents tend to interest themselves in only a very small local area.

If you think that your property will be particularly attractive to the non-French, and possibly to a particular nationality, you can use an agent in England or elsewhere. For a variety of reasons, this is not to be recommended except in the case of agents who have a proved long-term practical knowledge of French methods of dealing with sales and particulars of property.

You can try to sell without the use of an agent (known as *particulier à particulier* privately) but except in a large town this is probably not a good idea. Advertisements in English Sunday newspapers do produce results and save commission but you will be very much 'on your own' if you use this method, with no one to offer you advice.

No-one may carry on the business of an estate agent in France (whatever his nationality and whether he carries it on in France or from outside France) unles he holds a *carte professionnelle*. This is granted only to persons who can fulfil certain professional qualifications or can prove that they have had long experience in the field. In addition, they must be suitably bonded in respect of all moneys they will be holding on behalf of third parties. Certain other strict requirements are in force. It is worthwhile making certain that you are dealing with an agent, be he French or not, who complies with all these requirements.

The Mandat

No-one may deal with land transactions in France if he does not hold the prior written authority *(mandat)* of the person for whom he is acting. Each person instructing him must receive an original. Make certain that your *mandat* is fully signed and dated. Every *mandat* must be entered in a register in date order and the register number must figure on the copy given to the client. Failure to abide by the rules results in no commission for the agent and can lead to a term of imprisonment or a fine and the withrawal of a *carte professionnelle*.

Read with the greatest care any *mandat* you are asked to sign. It may be exclusive or non-exclusive and limited in time. Some are for a given period only; some are for an initial period and then run on until cancelled by the client. If they require cancellation, this must be done precisely in accordance with the stated provisions. The authority should state the minimum price at which the seller will sell and great care must be taken to ensure that the *mandat* does not include a specific power for the agent to sign a contract on behalf of the seller at that price. Indeed, it is often safer to exclude that power.

Be very careful about giving more than one *mandat* at a time even if each is non-exclusive or you may find yourself with two sets of commission on your hands. Equally, if you have given only one *mandat*, make certain that if you find a buyer through your own efforts, you are nevertheless not liable to commission under that *mandat*. These documents may look simple but they are full of hidden traps for those not used to them. It is generally accepted that apart from the good quality estate agents, the business lacks certain ethical standards.

Selling commission

Estate Agents commission is not on a scale basis but works

out currently at about 5%, sometimes inclusive and sometimes exclusive of TVA. It is usually open to some negotiation. However, be careful how the question of commission is dealt with. In most parts of France it is the seller who pays in full but you must enquire about this. Many agents suggest a selling price and then add on their commission and you sell at that higher price. You will then get the price net of commission although, of course, it is you who has the liability to pay the commission. This is not the same as buyers paying agents' commission, which except by local custom or special arrangement, they do not. (See Chapter 4.)

Commission is earned when contracts are signed. Virtually every contract states that the parties were introduced by XYZ estate agent as a result of which commission of a set amount is payable by the seller. Agents have found it necessary, in many standard forms of contract, to ask the parties to undertake that, if by mutual agreement they cancel the contract but then proceed to complete the transaction without informing the agent in the hope of avoiding the payment of commission, *both* parties will become liable to pay.

Preparing the contract

There is no reason why initially the agent should not prepare the contract but you are well-advised to have it checked by your local adviser before you sign it. In most cases, you do not need a notarial contract but if your agent produces anything other than a *compromis de vente*, make sure you have it checked. Your agent cannot properly prepare a contract without showing the *acte de vente* to you and, if you are selling a flat, your *règlement de copropriété*. If you have not got the *expedition* of your *acte de vente* (see Chapter 4), all you need to remember is the name of the notary who acted in the purchase and the date of the purchase. He will supply you with a further copy.

Normally, if you or your local adviser had no problems with the notary who acted for you on your purchase, insert his name as acting in the sale. Do not agree to a change of notary but, if the buyer wants to use an additional notary, then this is in order and both will be involved. In any event, sellers do not pay notarial fees.

Take note of the date shown in the contract. It is very rare for both parties to sign on the same date. This is important for both seller and buyer if the buyer is getting a mortgage, since the period during which the contract is conditional on the buyer getting the loan starts from the date of the contract.

Once the contract has been signed, send it (or a copy) to your notary. Although on a sale, local advice may seem less necessary than on a purchase, this is not always so. Your local adviser will organise the paper work with the notary, but if you think you can deal with a problem yourself, go and see him yourself and do not leave this to the agent.

The tax position

If you are selling your principle private residence in France, there will be no capital gains tax liability. It is extremely unlikely that you can use this exemption unless you are normally resident in France for all purposes. If you are not resident in France but are resident in England (among other countries), you should be exempt from capital gains tax on the first (but not on any subsequent) sale of a holiday home in France provided that you have used it only for your own occupation. Despite this exemption, at the time of writing, the French tax authorities are claiming that it causes too much work to check the entitlement to this exemption and are in many cases refusing it out of hand. How to deal with this situation as well as what to do where you would not be exempt, requires a notary acting for you who has experience of dealing with non-residents and if you have the slightest doubt about this, get separate advice.

If you are non-resident for tax purposes in France and cannot claim any exemptions, you will be liable to capital gains tax on the sale of your property if, of course, there is a taxable gain. Such a gain is calculated by reference to the purchase price plus the cost of purchase (always allowed at 10% of the price), to the extent of any allowable work you have carried out in the house (not including painting and decorating) and to the relevant inflation factor.

EXAMPLE

		FF
Price of flat bought in 1980		500,000
Add cost of purchase		50,000
Add cost of allowable works		100,000
		650,000
Inflation factor in 1990 for house bought in 1980		
1.78 × 650,000	=	1,157,000
Sale price in 1989		950,000

Therefore, since the sale price is less than the adjusted purchase price there is no CGT payable.

If you are non-resident, when you sell your French property you are required to appoint an *agent fiscale accredité* or guarantor for the payment of CGT. This is necessary irrespective of whether there is a CGT liability or, if there is, whether it has been calculated and paid out of the proceeds of sale. This is because the French Revenue has a period of four years in which it can reopen the calculation and ask for more tax. Such a guarantor may be a French bank: it will usually block a part of the sale price for as long as its guarantee is in force and it will charge a fee. However, this situation can be avoided if you adopt the correct procedure.

Before completion of a sale, an application must be made to the tax authorities for dispensation from the appointment of an *agent fiscal accredité*. This will normally be granted if there is clearly no CGT payable or if the amount of tax calculated to be due is accepted as correct. Such a dispensation must be requested even if you are on the face of it exempt from this tax. Then the proceeds of sale, in full or after payment of CGT, can be released to you and a considerable expense avoided. It is the duty of the notary acting for you to ask for this *dispense* and you, or your attorney if you have appointed one to act on the sale, should *never* complete without checking that it has been obtained.

So many misunderstandings arise over the liability to French CGT that it is worth repeating what has been said above. If you have the slightest doubt about the expertise of the notary dealing with your sale, *get advice from another source, preferably your local adviser whom you have appointed your attorney.*

Completion of the sale

This is the reverse of the situation when you buy. You should note the following points:

1   There is no reason why non-residents should not pay the price between themselves outside France. It is then a sale *hors vue de notaire.* Remember that if you have received the sale price in this way, you must have sufficient cash in France to be able to make the payments mentioned below, before or at completion. On the whole, there are likely to be problems in this type of sale if you or the buyer is resident in France for tax purposes.

2   If you are selling property *en copropriété*, it is the duty of the notary acting for you to obtain from the *syndic* a note of the service charges due from you to the date of sale and to pay these direct to the *syndic* out of the proceeds of sale. You will be asked to confirm the figure, which you cannot do exactly because no one knows what the final service charge figure will be but you should have a rough idea. Query it if you have any doubts. Obviously, it may turn out that the amount paid to the *syndic* was too much or too little. In England, it is the task of the solicitors involved to sort this out at the end of the service charge year. It is *not* the task of the notary to do this and very frequently nothing is ever done about it. However, if works to your block have been voted at a meeting of flat

owners before completion of the sale, you will be liable for this expense although it is incurred after you have sold the property. In such a case, someone will chase you for the cash in due course. Remember, however, that the *syndic* has a lien on the *whole* of the proceeds of sale in the hands of the notary, who cannot therefore pay out this money to you until outstanding service charges to the date of completion have been agreed and paid.

3   There are special rules about insurance on a sale. They are complicated but you need not worry about them. On completion, just make certain that it is agreed that you cancel your insurance on the property. You will have to do this yourself or get your local adviser to do it for you because it is not part of the notary's duty.

It is 100% certain that your estate agent will turn up at completion with his commission account. You will be asked to authorise payment which will be made out of the proceeds of sale. If an agent has received the deposit, he may not pay himself his commission out of it and account for the balance. He must bring the full amount to the notary on completion.

The Proceeds

Finally, you must accept that you will not get your proceeds of sale on the day of sale. How soon you will get them varies from notary to notary and depends on a number of factors but, on average, you should expect not to receive them for at least ten days. Make certain that you or your adviser checks with the notary when the payment is likely to be made and, if you are in a hurry, make certain he is aware of this. Since notaries do not keep clients' accounts in ordinary clearing banks, it seems impossible to arrange for payment to be made directly abroad. It will either be paid to your French bank account or through a French clearing bank to your account elsewhere, which will add to the delay in it reaching its correct destination.

20 The future

It is inevitable that a lot of what you have read in the preceding chapters may seem to be a series of warnings of what not to do, of things to avoid and of problems you will come up against. Do not be dismayed by this. There are a lot of things you would not be certain about if you were buying a house or a flat in the UK or trying to get planning consent to build your own house on a plot of land you had just bought. Some of the answers you need you can get for yourself because you speak the language fluently and because you know where to go to get them. The rest of your problems you would thankfully off-load on your solicitor, accountant and bank manager.

The difficulty when you buy property in France is that even if you are fluent in the language, the system simply does not provide you with advice as you go along as it does in England. Where it does give you advice, it is likely to do so on the assumption that you are French. You should therefore think of all that this book has told you not just as a series of pitfalls and difficulties but as an indication of how the French deal with property transactions. After all, there is no better way to enjoy a country than to understand its ways and no more certain way to be irritated by it than not to understand its citizens. The solution lies in trying to cope yourself with all that is involved in property transactions in France and to get from the outset proper advice from the right person.

It is obvious that anyone who owns a house in a foreign country, whether to live there permanently or only for a holiday, bought it because they were looking for a way of life different from that 'at home'. It is not likely that they will be disappointed with their choice of a home in France and it is hoped that this book will have helped in that choice. In the right parts, the climate is delightful. Almost the whole of the country is a gastronomic pasture, and if you listen to the local expert, you will drink well. France produces some of the finest dairy produce in the world and the fruit and vegetables at the local market are a joy to see and eat.

As to the inhabitants of the country, Philip Holland in his book *Living in France* sums it up admirably — 'The French character is different and complex. Sometimes it delights. Sometimes it puzzles. On occasion, it can provide surprises . . . The draw to foreigners lies in France's unique combination of people, history, geography, architecture and the variety of her countryside and climate. Most of the time the French really do try to live up to their motto *Liberté, Egalité, Fraternité,* if not always to the letter at least in spirit'.

Glossary

Most of the words which are explained below appear in the text but it is sometimes useful when faced with a technical word to be able to find its meaning easily. Dictionaries always need the most careful use and technical dictionaries more than most.

Treat any translation of a French legal document with much circumspection. Never sign one, but insist on signing only its original in French. It requires immense skill to make correct translations of legal documents and a complete knowledge of two sets of laws. If you sign a translation and then give it to your professional adviser, he will almost certainly tell you that it means nothing in English. Either the French technical terms will have been mistranslated; or if a 'correct' translation into English legal terms has been achieved, these terms when applied to French legal situations will have totally different meanings. Beware also some French technical terms which do not have meanings which you would expect them to have.

Acte de vente/achat A conveyance or transfer of land. It is usually called an *acte de vente* by both buyer or seller but *acte d'achat* is likewise sometimes used

Agence commercial The local telephone Manager's office

Agence fiscal accredité (See *Plus value*)

Agence immobilière Estate agent

AR letter All recorded delivery letters in France must be also registered at some considerable expense. Many notices etc must be sent by AR post but it is advisable to send any letter to which you want an immediate reply to in this way.

Arrhes   (See *Deposit*)

Attestation d'acquisition   A notarial certificate that you have completed the purchase of property

Bail   is a lease

Banque de consignation   The state bank at which notaries are obliged to keep clients' money and which does not provide either the client or the notary with interest

Bureau des hypothèques   Strictly this is one part of the French Land Registry, the other part being *cadastre* but loosely it covers both

Carte de séjour = permis de séjour   The permit issued by the French government authorising a person not of French nationality to reside in France.

Carte professionnelle   The authority issued by the *Préfecture* to (among others) estate agents authorising them to carry on business. Its issue implies that the holder has attained certain (often not very high) qualifications, is bonded for clients' money received by him and has effected professional indemnity cover.

Certificat de conformité   Either the certificate required by EDF (see below) before linking up a house or flat to the electricity supply or the certificate given to confirm that building has been completed in accordance with a Planning Consent

Certificat d'urbanisme   The reply to a planning search

Charges   Service charges

Commune   Local district varying from tiny village to large town

Compensable   means the clearing of a cheque

Compromis de vente   Contract for sale and purchase of land

Compte à terme   Deposit account

Compte courant   Current account

Concierge   (See *Gardien*)

Constat   A report made by a Hussier (see below)

Constructible   Land which is designated for building under local planning scheme

Contract de réservation   The purchase contract used for purchase 'on plan'

Contract préliminaire   A *contract de réservation* is sometimes so called

Copropriété   Co-ownership, usually of land eg flats are bought *en copropriété* but also of other assets such as boats

Deposit   Usually 10% of the purchase price and should be paid not to the seller's estate agent but either to the seller's notary or better to the notary to act for the buyer. If the words 'arrhes' or 'dedit' appear in the contract, seek advice since these are special types of deposits with unexpected results

Droits de succession/donation   Inheritance tax/Gift tax

EDF/GDF   Electricité de France/Gaz de France

Emoulements   a notary's scale fee

Enregistrement   Best, but not quite accurately translated as Stamp Duty

Etat des lieux   Schedule of Condition or Schedule of Dilapidations depending on whether it applies to the beginning or the end of a lease

Etat futur d'achèvement   Applies to a purchase 'on plan'

Eventuel   means possible or probable eg *un acquéreur eventuel* means a possible buyer

Expédition   The certified copy of a notarial document showing the date of its registration and the stamp duty paid

Expert comptable   (Chartered) accountant

Expert foncier   The French do not use surveyors as do the British to report on the state and value of property — they would use an architect. There are a few English Chartered Surveyors in France and it is worthwhile making use of them

Expertiser   To value

Feuille de soins   A form provided by a doctor, hospital, chemist etc covering treatment, drugs and the like recoverable in whole or part from Securité Social

FNAIM   Federation nationale des Agents Immobilier. It provides a compensation fund for defaulting agents

Fonds de roulement   Strictly this means 'working capital'. In connection with the management of blocks of flats, it means a kitty contributed to by all flat-owners in addition to their service charges to enable the Managing Agents to meet unexpected liabilities.

Fortune   is not wealth but capital

Foyer   Strictly speaking 'hearth' but technically for French tax purposes it has a rather wider meaning in that if your family sits round your hearth in France even if you are frequently absent, you may find yourself liable to French tax

Frais d'acte   See *Frais de notaire*

Frais de notaire   The *total* amount to be paid to the notary acting for the seller of property in addition to the sale price ie his scale fee, Stamp Duty, Land Registry fees and other disbursements and (in certain cases) the seller's commission. Usually, the notarial fee for the preparation of the sale document is a very small proportion of the total *frais*

France Télécom   The French British Telecom

Gardien(ne)   The modern name for concierge. The all important Head Porter or Portress of a block of flats

Honoraires   Professional fees not calculated by scale

Hopital conventioné   French National Health hospital

HT hors taxe   meaning ex-VAT

Hussier   Among his duties are those of a Sheriff's Officer, Bailiff and Process Server but he can be used to make reports on situations eg leaking roofs, damage to property or in other situations where proceedings are contemplated and it is desired to record evidence

Important   means large (amounts)

Indivision   The method of joint ownership roughly equivalent to English tenancy in common

Ligne mixte   A telephone line capable of being used to make and receive calls

Location   is a letting

Loi Scrivener   The law protecting borrowers from French lenders and sellers on French property purchases in all cases other than a purchase 'on plan'

Lotissement   Most easily translated as a building estate but with legal consequences rather different from those in England

Lots   (Land Registry plots) In blocks of flats or other condominiums, the non-common parts are divided into numbered lots which are used to describe the various private parts sold.

MPOA   Mediterranean Property Owners Association

Mairie   Town Hall even if the village population numbers no more than a hundred or so

Mandat   Agency agreement or Power of Attorney or generally an authority to someone to act on behalf of another

Monuments historiques   Listed buildings

Mutuel   Mutual benefit society to which it is frequently obligatory to belong

Offre d'achat/de vente   An offer to buy or sell property which is not of itself a binding contract but which is often

wished on buyers or sellers as a sort of 'holding' situation.
Not to be accepted without independent advice

Permis de construire   Planning consent

Pharmacie de garde   Duty chemist

Plus value   (Capital gains tax) The non-resident owner of
property in France may be required on its sale to appoint an
agent fiscal accredité to be responsible for CGT

POS   Planning Scheme

Pouvoir   Mandate

Prélèvement   Direct debit

Prise en charge   An undertaking (usually provided by the
DSS of Form E112) to be responsible for French hospital
fees so that one need not pay these and recover them
subsequently in the UK

Provision   applies technically to the state of your bank
account. A cheque *sans provision* is a cheque which your bank
cannot or will not meet for lack of funds

Rejeter   To 'bounce' a cheque

Réservation   The deposit in a *contract de réservation* (see
above). It is not a deposit 'to reserve' a property and is not
normally returnable unless the seller is in default

Réservation, contract de   The type of contract for the
purchase of property *état d'achèvement futur* (see above)
which must follow certain strict requirements

Résiliation   Cancellation of a contract

SAFER   A local quasi-government organisation whose duty
is to ensure the proper use of agricultural land. Hence such
land is often subject to a SAFER right to buy in on any sale
and on many sales in the country, it is necessary to obtain the
local SAFER's agreement not to exercise its powers of pre-
emption. Also, many SAFERs can be subject to local politics
and minor corruption

Securité sociale   French National Health Scheme

Société Company but not always providing limited liability

Statuts The Memorandum of Articles of a French *société*

Syndic The Managing Agent of a *copropriété*

TTC toutes taxes comprise meaning VAT inclusive

TVA Taxe sur la valuer ajoutée meaning VAT

Tantième The proportion of the common parts of a *copropriété* owned jointly with other flat-owners by any given flat. It is the basic factor in the calculation of Service Charges and a flat-owners voting rights

Taxe d'habitation General rates levied on the occupation of property

Taxe foncière Local tax levied on the ownership of property

Testament will of which there are three types. Never try to make one without proper legal advice which is best obtained from one person expert in both English and French law

Timbre fiscal Certain documents such as applications for a *carte de séjour* carry a Revenue Stamp

Tontine The method of joint ownership roughly equivalent to English joint tenancy.

Troisième age Senior citizen. Cf. *retraité* and *pré-retraité* which are officially recognised statuses in France and continuously dreamt of by every employee from the day he or she takes his or her first job.

Index

Acte de vente, 24, 28–29
Advice—
  being prepared to seek, 3
  legal, 20
  wills, 118
Airports, 12–13
Annual taxes, 59, 63–4
Architect—
  discussion with, 50–2
Assurance Automatique Acquéreur, 25–6
Authentic will, 115

Banks—
  accounts—
    cheques, 55–6
    current, 54
    deposit, 54
    direct debits, 56–7
    opening, 54
    property purchase loans, 57
    protection of borrower, 57–58
  drafts, 55
  generally, 53–4
  UK Branches, 53–54
  See also Cheques
Britanny, 10
Budgeting, 17–18
Building—
  completion of, 35–6
  contracts, 17
  do-it-yourself—
    certificat de conformité, 46–7
    certificate d'urbanisme, 46
    permis de construire, 46
    plan d'occupation des sols, 45
  new property—
    architect, discussion with, 50–2

Building—*contd*
  new property—*contd*
    do-it-yourself, 45–7
    generally, 43–4
    methods, 47–9
    planning, 44–5
    what not to buy, 49–50
Buying on plan—
  advantages, 32
  completion of building, 35–6
  purchase contract, 32–5
Buying process—
  budgeting, 17–18
  completion, 29–31
  contract, 22–6
  conveyance, 28–9
  dos and don'ts, 16–21
  finance, *see* Financing purchase
  generally, 22
  house purchase loans, 27–8, 57
  inspection, 19
  legal side, 20
  seller's commission, 26–7
  taxation, 20–21
  what to buy, 6–8

Capital gains tax, 59, 64
Car, 89
Carte de séjour, 88
Certificat de conformité, 46–7
Certificat de perte, 102
Certificate d'urbanisme, 46
Chateau, 6, 8
Cheques—
  bearer, 55
  bouncing, 56
  ordinary, 55–6

Cheques—*contd*
  postdated, 55
  stopping, 55
Climate, 5–6
Code numbers of départements, 15
Commission—
  contract clause, 24
  seller, of, 26–7
  selling, 125–8
Companies—
  insurance, 100–2
  offshore, 67
  time-sharing, 71–3
Completion—
  building, of, 35–6
  clauses, 34–35
  buying process, 29–31
  payment, 30–31
  dates, 24–5
  selling property, 130–1
  statement, 30
Condominium—
  costs of ownership, 74–5
  dos and don'ts, 78
  generally, 74
  liabilities, 76–7
  life in, 74–81
  management of block, 78–9
  meetings, 79–81
  members absent from meetings, 81
  obligations, 76–7
  service charges, 77–8
  systems of ownership, 75–6
Contract—
  building, 17
  buying on plan, 32–5
  compromis de vente, 23
  preparation of, 22–6, 127–128
  purchase, 32–5
  signing, 28
Conveyance, 28–9
Costs—
  flat ownership, 74–5
  maintenance, 99–100
  time-sharing, 69–70
Côte d'Azur, 9
Counties, *see* Départements
Currency considerations, 41–2
Current accounts, 54

Death—
  provision for, 108
  succession law, 109–12

Death—*contd*
  See also Wills
Départements—
  code numbers, 15
Deposit accounts, 54
Deposits, 23–4
Direct debits, 56–7
Do-it-yourself—
  certificat de conformité, 46–7
  certificate d'urbanisme, 46
  permis de construire, 46
  plan d'occupation des sols, 45
Domicile, 61
Dordogne, 10
Double tax treaty, 59
Duty-free goods—
  importing, 90–1

Electricity, 94–5
Enregistrement, 61–2
Estate agents, 125
Exchange control—
  banking, 53–4
  mortgage, 18
Executors, 116–7

Financing property—
  currency considerations, 41–2
  English property used as security, 40–1
  French property used as security, 39–40
  generally, 37–8
  See also Loans; Mortgage
Flats—
  buying on plan—
    advantages, 32
    completion of building, 35–6
    purchase contract, 32–5
  elderly, catering for, 107
  ownership—
    costs, 74–5
    dos and don'ts, 78
    liabilities, 76–7
    management of block, 78–9
    meetings, 79–81
    members absent from meetings, 81
    obligations, 76–7
    systems of, 75–6
  service charges, 25, 77–8
  swimming pools, 12
  what to buy, 6–7
Frauds, 1

Future, 132–3

Gas, 95, 96
Glossary, 135–41

Health—
 death, provision for, 108
 holiday insurance for tourists, 103
 medical insurance, 106–8
 reciprocal medical care, 103–4
 residents, of, 105
 Sécurité Sociale, 106
Holiday—
 insurance, 103
 lettings, 119–20
Holograph will, 115, 116
House purchase, *see* Buying process
House-hunting, 12

Identity papers, 89
Importing duty-free goods, 90–1
Income tax, 64
Inheritance tax, 59, 64–6, 117
Inspection of property, 19
Insurance—
 arranging, 16
 Assurance Automatique Acquéreur, 25–6
 company, 100–2
 holiday, 103
 medical, 106–8
 renting property, 84–5
 settling in, 92
Intention of book, 1

Land tax, 31
Legal advice, 20
Letting property—
 general guidelines, 122–3
 holidays, 119–20
 long-term, 122
 rules of, 120–1
 See also Renting property
Loans—
 house purchase, 27–8, 57
 protection of borrower, 58
 See also Financing property
Long-term lettings, 122

Maintenance, 99–100
Management of block, 78–9
Mas, 6, 7–8
Medical care—
 insurance, 106–8

Medical care—*contd*
 reciprocal, 103–4
 residents, for, 105
Meetings—
 flat owners, 79–81
 members absent from, 81
Monaco, 13–14
Mortgage—
 arrangements, 16
 protection of borrower, 58
 See also Financing property
Moving—
 making move, 89–90
 removal firm, use of, 91
Mystic will, 116

New property, *see* Building
Normandy, 10
Notarial will, 115

Office of Fair Trading, 70
Offshore companies, 67

Papers, 89
Permanent residence—
 application for, 87–8
Permis de construire, 46
Plan, buying on, *see* Buying on plan
Plan d'occupation des sols, 45
Planning—
 new property, 44–5
Property—
 letting, *see* Letting property
 purchase of, *see* Buying process
 renting, *see* Renting property
 selling, *see* Selling property
Protection of borrower, 58
Provence, 9
Purchase contract—
 buying on plan, 32–5

Railway system, 13
Reciprocal medical care, 103–4
Removal firm—
 use of, 91
Renting property—
 generally, 82
 insurance, 84–5
 points to note, 83–4
 repairs, 84
 service charges, 85–6
 See also Letting property

Repairs—
  renting property, 84
Réserve, 114–15
Residence—
  permanent, application for, 87–8
  taxation, 60
Residents—
  medical provision for, 105
Road travel, 13
Running costs, 99–100

Searches, 24, 25
Secret will, 116
Sécurité Sociale, 106
Security—
  English property used as, 40–1
  French property used as, 39–40
Seller's commission, 26–7
Selling property—
  completion of sale, 130–1
  estate agents, 125
  generally, 124
  proceeds of sale, 131
  sale price, 124
  selling commission, 126–8
  tax position, 128–30
Service charges—
  buying process, 25
  flat owners, 25, 77–8
  renting property, 85–6
Settling in—
  car, 89
  generally, 87
  identity papers, 89
  importing duty-free goods, 90–1
  insurance, 92
  making move, 89–90
  permanent residence, 87–8
  removal firm, 91
Sewage, 99
Stamp duties, 59, 61–2
Succession law, 109–12

TVA, 59, 62–3
Taxation—
  annual taxes, 59, 63–4
  capital gains tax, 59, 64
  domicile, 61
  double tax treaty, 59
  enregistrement, 61–2
  income tax, 64
  inheritance tax, 59, 64–6, 117
  land tax, 31

Taxation—*contd*
  offshore companies, 67
  property purchase, 20–1
  residence, 60
  selling property, 128–30
  stamp duties, 59, 61–2
  value added tax, 59, 62–3
  wealth tax, 60
Telephone, 96–8
Television, 99
Time-sharing—
  costs, 69–70
  generally, 68–9
  guidelines, 70
  old system v new system, 71–3
Title deeds, 23, 31
Tourists—
  holiday insurance, 103
Travelling, 12–14

Utilities—
  electricity, 94–5
  gas, 95, 96
  sewage, 99
  telephone, 96–8
  television, 99
  water, 93–4

Value added tax, 59, 62–3
Visa de longue durée, 88

Warnings, 3–4
Water, 93–4
What to buy, 6–8
Where to buy—
  Britanny, 10
  climate, 5–6
  Côte d'Azur, 9
  Dordogne, 10
  how to get there, 12–14
  Normandy, 10
  Provence, 9
  what to buy, 6–8
  when to house-hunt, 12
Wills—
  advice on, 118
  authentic, 115
  executors, 116–17
  generally, 113
  holograph, 115, 116
  how many, 113–14
  inheritance tax, 117

Wills—*contd*
    making, 113–18
    mystic, 116
    notarial, 115
    réserve, 114–15

Wills—*contd*
    secret, 116
    succession law, 109–12
    two, 114
    types of, 115–16

Other titles in the Allied Dunbar Library
Allied Dunbar Money Guides

- Buying Your Home   Richard Newell
- Financial Care for Your Elderly Relatives   Beverly Chandler
- Financial Planning for the Over 50s   Rober Leach
- Insurance: Are you Covered?   Mihir Bose
- Investing in Shares   Hugh Pym & Nick Kochan
- Leaving Your Money Wisely   Tony Foreman
- Making Your Job Work   David Williams
- Managing Your Finances   Helen Pridham
- Planning School and College Fees   Danby Block & Amanda Pardoe
- Planning Your Pension   Tony Reardon
- Tax and Finance for Women   Helen Pridham
- Tax for the Self-Employed   David Williams
- Your Home in Italy   Flavia Maxwell
- Your Home in Portugal   Rosemary de Rougemont
- Your Home in Spain   Per Svensson

All of these titles in the Allied Dunbar Library are available from leading bookshops

For more information please contact: Longman Law, Tax and Finance, 21—27 Lamb's Conduit St, LONDON WC1N 3NJ
Tel: (071) 242 2548